Living With Your Psychic Gifts

---

*Written by Brandi Jasmine,
with help from John Nemanic*

Living With Your Psychic Gifts

Written by Brandi Jasmine, with John Nemanic
www.psychicprotection.net

Published by Nalanda Publishing

ISBN 0-9732865-0-4

Version 2, Copyright 2015, Brandi Jasmine,
All Rights Reserved
Cover illustration and design by Brandi Jasmine,
Copyright 2015, All Rights Reserved

Dedicated to my Angels. You know who you are.

Living With Your Psychic Gifts

Contents

Chapter One:	How Did You Realize You Were Psychic?
Chapter Two:	Am I Crazy? Or Just Showing Signs Of A Psychic Gift?
Chapter Three:	Psychic Protection & Other Meditation Tips
Chapter Four:	Controlling Psychic Growth
Chapter Five:	Dreams, OOBEs, Auras, The Etheric Body And The Astral Plane
Chapter Six:	Shocking Experiences ("Kundalini")
Chapter Seven:	Addressing Concerns Of Family, Friends & Church
Chapter Eight:	Dealing With Psychic Children
Chapter Nine:	Finding A Good Psychic First – Know Thyself
Chapter Ten:	"The Occult"
Chapter Eleven:	Ghosts, Spirits, Channeling
Chapter Twelve:	The Circle Meditation
Chapter Thirteen:	Personal Growth & Psychic Ability
Chapter Fourteen:	Doing Readings, Going Professional

Glossary

Introduction

Psychic phenomena is big business these days, what with the plethora of 900 instant psychics and the palm & tarot readers popping up on every city street corner. There are many books, magazines and articles written by psychics. Psychics are now regular visitors on mainstream talk shows, and there are even highly popular cable TV shows entirely dedicated to psychics. There are hundreds of thousands of psychic, astrological and metaphysical websites.

It wasn't always so acceptable to discuss psychic phenomena. In long periods of human history, it was so taboo that confessing to psychic experiences could lead to torture and a death sentence. In modern times, admitting to having psychic experiences is still likely to lead to ridicule from peers and friends, or the dangers associated with being labeled mentally ill. While "professional" psychics are regular features on talk and entertainment television, it is still rare to hear from ordinary people who have their own psychic experiences. Most people are still too afraid of ridicule and censure to share these experiences too openly, and they believe that this is a rare occurrence, something that happens to someone else, someone highly spiritual (whatever that may mean to them).

Living With Your Psychic Gifts

In reality though, the experience is actually quite common. Millions of people have had psychic experiences of one form or another. In one online poll I conducted, over 85% of respondents indicated they had some kind of psychic experience. It is only in modern times that people have felt comfortable enough to come forward to talk about these experiences, and even now, the old taboos keep many silent. Many people are led to question their own sanity before they find the courage to seek out information about these experiences.

What information a person can access depends greatly on religious, political and cultural expectations. If you are raised, as I was, in a fundamentalist Christian family, you can add condemnation, alienation from loved ones, and fears of demon possession to fears of madness. The impact on your psychological and emotional well being can be devastating.

Then there are the frauds. There are so many deceptive "psychics", from the scripted "cold reader" to well-meaning but ultimately self-deceived charlatans, that a sincere seeker is always questioning the reality of what they experience.

A confused, frightened person facing an unwelcome psychic experience faces a challenging gauntlet of cultural neurosis and hostility before they get to the heart of the matter: "Is this real? Am I crazy?" "Does anyone else have this happening to them?" and "Am I alone?"

I asked myself these questions when I first began to consciously explore psychic experiences in the early 1980's. I felt completely alone, confused and dismayed by a series of psychic events that left me questioning everything I believed about my religion, culture, and the nature of reality itself. I was raised in a fundamentalist Pentecostal religion. To say I was horrified at the time doesn't begin to do justice to my feelings back then. But I needed to know what was happening. Was this real? Was I losing my mind?

I quickly discovered that there was a vast amount of "pop culture" material to read about pop culture psychics. But there was little practical, real-life guidance for an honest seeker, especially not if you wanted to turn it off. There were no wise gurus, no "Obi-Wan Kenobi" to guide me on my search, just a plethora of wordy and confusing out of date books, over-priced "intensive" Kundalini workshops and the obligatory charlatan waiting in the wings to take my money and waste my time.

Living With Your Psychic Gifts

Eventually, with the help of some caring mentors and fellow seekers, I began to understand that what was happening was not evil, wrong or delusional. After I got my feet back on the ground, and felt more comfortable with the label "psychic", I began to offer readings to others.

I originally wrote *Living With Your Psychic Gifts* because a large number of my clients were looking for information about their own psychic experiences. They would come to me with headaches, anxiety attacks, mood-swings, undiagnosed medical problems and nightmares, but it was the psychic visions seemed to distress them the most. I could recommend six or seven books ... but no one single reference booklet that they could read that hit the target, to help them come to grips with this life-altering experience. I wanted to be a source of help and support for them, something I did not have, when I began my spiritual journey. One of my greatest joys are the emails I get from readers who tell me they no longer feel so alone. I know exactly how that feels.

Living With Your Psychic Gifts

Who can benefit from reading this book?

Sometimes people are born with psychic talents. Everyone knows sensitive children who you can't fool, no matter what. A rueful mother is heard to exclaim "That child reads my mind!" A small number grow up supported and encouraged by parents who also have such talents, or come from culturally supportive backgrounds, but the vast majority learn that parents, siblings and peers fear their strange abilities. They learn to hide those insights, pushing feelings and insights deep under the veil of consciousness. But the talent bursts forth again later on in life, forcing them to face the fact that something unusual is going on. Sometimes a relationship or personal tragedy is foreseen. Others have shocking near-death or out of body experiences. Often they have accidentally left themselves "wide open" psychically after a workshop, lecture, meditation seminar or intense prayer.

What may start off as a periodic trickle of "strange coincidences" turns into a flood of bizarre, sometimes frightening experiences that leaves a person bewildered and confused. It is a difficult state of mind, people in our culture are only rarely prepared to deal with it, and many people are frightened to speak out to anyone else for fear of ridicule, censure or worse.

That fear is not unreasonable. Even in these supposedly enlightened times, no-one wants to be associated with the often laughably silly 900-line "psychics" that litter the entertainment landscape. Though there have been a number of credible big-name psychics as well, it is the "entertainment" variety most people seem to best remember. The average person does not want to be lumped into that crowd. Worse, many people associate psychic experiences with insanity. There can be associations with mental illness in some rare cases, but the main risk a psychic faces is the understandable depression and emotional trauma that comes from living with a strange experience that no one else seems to want to talk about or understand. An already highly sensitive person can find this challenge completely overwhelming.

These days, psychic phenomena is becoming mainstream. There are many other books written about psychic abilities now, and I am glad to see them. Many of these books are directed at serious scholars or students of metaphysics though, and a lot of them are written with so much pseudo-scientific metaphysical jargon or occult mumbo-jumbo that your head is spinning by the time you finish the introduction. Those that are written for the layperson seem to be directed to expanding rather than controlling psychic ability, or are directed exclusively to the "Pop Culture" or entertainment market. Supermarket tabloid astrology booklets are a good example of this genre. They are fun and entertaining, but they are vague, and contain little practical information. Either way, wading through the volumes of information to find one simple, straightforward, and easy to read book on the subject can be a daunting task.

In *Living With Your Psychic Gifts*, I have distilled the simplest, most effective ideas, concepts and exercises into a concise, easy to read book that covers the bases and provides simple exercises for anyone wanting to learn to understand and control unwanted or unexpected psychic activity. By no means is this book the end of the journey – it is only the beginning. But it is meant to be comforting and reassuring, practical and easy to understand, a starting place to help you cope with an experience you did not ask for, and may have found disturbing, frightening or confusing.

While you travel your pathway to better understanding, you'll meet a lot of people who set themselves before you as "teachers", "healers", "psychics" and "gurus". Remember that almost none of these people are trained formally. Few of them have much if any medical, legal or psychological training (and that includes me). If you are presented with ideas that don't make sense – challenge the source. Ask questions. Don't allow anyone to demand your unquestioning faith. If a thing does not make sense, throw it out. Take what you can, what makes sense, and abandon those parts that don't ring true for you. Trust yourself.

There are now some teachers traveling the lecture circuit, teaching "psychic development" courses. Before you attend such courses, ask questions. Remember that some people presenting themselves as "experts" on the lecture circuit have little experience with psychic trouble. This path comes easily to them, and they often assume it works that way for everyone. Insist on being taught some basic psychic protection before you are shown any meditation or visualization technique designed to heighten psychic sensitivity. If anyone tells you that you don't need psychic protection, walk away. What they are teaching is not for anyone who identifies as sensitive.

Get a check-up

Before starting a new exercise routine or diet you would check with your doctor, and if you believe you may be psychic, it is only prudent to rule out medical problems before you start a psychic exercise program.

Many of the signs and symptoms of psychic awakening coincide with, or resemble the signs of physical, emotional and/or psychological disorders. You cannot say that you are certain your experiences are "psychic" until you rule out other possible causes.

ALWAYS SEEK OUT THE CARE OF A QUALIFIED DOCTOR, NATUROPATH AND/OR THERAPIST IN CONJUNCTION WITH ANY ALTERNATIVE THERAPIES OR PRACTICES YOU UNDERTAKE.

I no longer do many in-person psychic readings because I find that it opens up my aura to too many unwanted psychic energies. Back when I was doing readings, many clients came during a time of crisis because they were reluctant to seek medical or psychological help. They feared being labeled "crazy". Today, many of the

Living With Your Psychic Gifts

emails I get come from readers of *Living With Your Psychic Gifts* who express these and similar concerns. I understand, because when I was struggling with my own psychic gifts, I worried about that too. It can be difficult to find a doctor who is open minded when discussing the possibility of psychic ability.

My own worst fears were confirmed when one doctor, upon learning of my new work as a psychic, stifled a smirk and said: "So when did you start hearing voices?" The fact that I never heard "voices" was beside the point to him. It was shortly after that encounter that I found myself a new doctor.

The risk of a bad experience can pale in comparison with the alternative, however. There are some symptoms that can have both psychic and physical or psychological causes, and it is vital to have these causes ruled out.

Never abandon medical advice on the suggestion of a psychic or spiritual teacher. If you are not comfortable confiding fully in your doctor, you may choose to keep your ideas about the psychic origins of your symptoms to yourself, or describe them in completely psychological or medical terms, but if you are experiencing dizziness, nausea, disassociation (feeling like you are floating out of the body), headaches or other physical signs, or are experiencing frightening emotional symptoms like anxiety, paranoia, or indeed do hear voices (especially if they are negative and tell you to do bad things), don't wait. See a doctor!

If your question is not answered in this book ...

I have an open discussion group on my web site at www.psychicprotection.net where I answer questions and participate in ongoing discussions (as time permits). I am also available for questions about psychic experiences on the *Living With Your Psychic Gifts* Facebook Page at www.facebook.com/psychicprotection.

I do not charge a fee to answer individual questions about psychic growth or development, provided they are asked in the public groups and are new questions not answered in the book or the FAQ. It may take between a few hours and a few days between responses, depending on whether I am at home or on the road.

I do offer private psychic development consultations and coaching. Answers to public questions help not only the person asking them, but also all readers with the same issues. And nearly all the private questions I get are in fact answered in *Living With Your Psychic Gifts* or its online FAQs. I understand that some people feel the need for privacy and anonymity, and it takes time to read the whole book and FAQ for answers. It is only fair that those wanting private attention, or a short-cut to their answer, contribute something so that those who do share in public continue to have a place to share and learn.

Living With Your Psychic Gifts Lectures & Workshops

If you are looking for a speaker on the topic of psychic gifts, contact me at:

www.psychicprotection.net

Chapter One
How Did You Realize You Were Psychic?

This is the most frequent question I am asked when people learn that I used to work as a full-time "psychic" (I prefer "intuitive consultant"). It is not as easy to answer as it might seem. In my family, the events that I would later understand as "psychic" were considered signs of "emotional over-sensitivity" or the signs of an active imagination. It was not until my early twenties when I realized that something more than imagination was active in my life.

It was on a strange New Years Day in my early 20's that I met someone who was destined to be the catalyst for the experiences that would change my life. We met in a smoky, dark, loud, local dance club. We fell in love with each other's minds at first, talking the nights away for several days before the relationship became romantic. I remember him telling me that a psychic had told him he would meet someone special that night. I laughed. After all, I didn't believe in psychics. It was nonsense at best, and evil at worst to consult with wizards and fortunetellers. He dropped the subject for a time, and we got on with the more interesting business of getting to know each other.

Living With Your Psychic Gifts

I never felt so connected to someone. It was as if I could read his thoughts. I could tell where he was and who he was with, what he was doing, even from across town. I could find him in any of the dozen or so places we frequented, even when he was supposed to be somewhere else. It did not occur to me consciously at the time that this was something "psychic", I assumed that this was a manifestation of love.

One day, I felt an overwhelming urge to go and find him. I felt that something awful had happened, and I couldn't reach him anywhere. Desperate, I searched everywhere, for the first time finding it difficult to locate him. Finally I found him, calmly sitting with some friends at a bar. When I went to tell him of the experience, he seemed unpleasantly surprised. He told me that the "message" he sent was meant for someone else, and dismissed me rather harshly to wonder about this latest strange episode in my life. He disappeared for a month after that. While he was missing, my frequent headaches and dizzy spells were increasing.

One day, walking down the street, I felt the now familiar ticking on top of my head. The image of a man, with dark hair and a thin face popped into my mind. I seemed to sense that he had an odd accent of some kind, and I could understand what he seemed to want to say to me. There was no "voice in my head", rather, a sensation much like that of remembering a conversation I had never heard. His name was "David Y", and he said he was a friend of the young man I had been seeing.

I immediately dismissed the experience. I remember thinking "Okay, you are stressed out, and now you are losing your mind!" But the experience ended as quickly as it began, and it did not return to trouble me. I resolved to put it out of my mind.

Then one day, the young man's mother called. By this time she was frantic. He had been missing for nearly a month. Did I know where he was? I didn't know, but as we talked she brought up the subject of the psychic he had seen so many months ago. On an impulse, I described the man in my vision. She did not seem surprised. "Oh, that's David Y. Do you know him?"

I was stunned. I had not known of this man, who turned out to be a well-known and popular television medium with a strong reputation for accuracy. In my family background though, consulting a psychic was unthinkable, and I had never heard of him before. Now, however, I had to find out more about him. It turned out that he was on TV shortly afterward. I was shocked once again. It was the exact same man I had "seen" in my mind!

I felt more alone and frightened than ever. I could not confide my experiences to anyone in my circle of family and friends. They would think I was crazy, or demon possessed. I waited until finally, my boyfriend returned. I never did receive an explanation from him. His last words spoken to me were an unprintable profanity, and he never spoke to me again.

I only once tried to speak to "David Y", a few months later. A warm flush of electrical energy came over my head and I could only stammer that I would call him back. I was too terrified to say anything to him, and I never tried again.

To this day, I do not know for certain why the young man acted as he did, only that he left me in an open and vulnerable psychic state, and that there was more yet to come.

In the months that followed, my friends began to take an interest in the new talent that I was exhibiting. They wanted me to display my "gift" at parties and get-togethers. I was not comfortable with all the attention, however. I did not want to be called "psychic". I resolved to put the experiences out of my mind, and to get on with my life.

Unfortunately though, the experiences began to take on a more menacing tone. I began to experience bizarre nightmares. I would wake up in the middle of a dream, aware that I was dreaming, but unable to wake up. My body would be paralyzed. I heard rushing noises in my ears, and heat in my forearms. I would scream out to the only source of protection I knew, but not even Jesus would come to my aid. I woke, night after night, terrified, and drenched in sweat.

I went from doctor to doctor, trying to find a reason for the dreams, the headaches, the vibrations. "There's nothing wrong with you. You are just stressed, take some anti-depressants." I began to wonder if I was truly losing my mind.

Finally I confided some of my visions and dreams to my mother. A fundamentalist Christian, she was upset by this revelation, and urged me to go to church. I had been praying for answers for a long time. I wanted the Lord to show me the truth, and I wanted deliverance from the nightmares that by this time were coming night after night, so I went to church.

Living With Your Psychic Gifts

The sermon was "Visions and Dreams, How God Communicates with You."

I figured if this could happen in a church, it had to be a sign that whatever was happening, it was okay with God. Delighted to have received such a powerful message, I resolved to discover more about this gift. I began to explore the Bible, but the more I read the more questions I needed to explore. Why was there such denunciation of psychic abilities when the prophets themselves use what seems to be the same gift? The standard answers did not satisfy me. The more I read the Bible and studied Christian teachings, the more disillusioned I became. I resolved to cast a wider net in my search for the truth about these strange experiences.

One day, I stumbled into a large "new-age" bookstore. I was still confused and frightened. The "Experiences" as I call them were almost nightly occurrences. By this time, I was beginning to wonder how good a grip I held on reality. The woman behind the counter was so friendly that she immediately put me at ease. She accepted my religious beliefs, even though she was into the teachings of an eastern guru. I was skeptical. After all, my whole life I had read about these "false prophets" and their teachings, how they were dangerous cults, and spent time and money brainwashing people.

Still, here was this woman, friendly and understanding, where others had reacted with nervousness or derisive humor. She put me in touch with a fellow named Elliot, who she said "Knew something about psychic and Kundalini experiences".

I had never heard of "Kundalini", but by this time, I was desperate. I called. Elliot patiently explained psychic energy to me over a long phone conversation, and gave me the advice that I now believe may have saved my life. He told me there was nothing to fear, just dip my feet in cold water whenever I had an uncomfortable "vibration" sensation.

Gradually, the "Experiences" grew less frequent and more pleasant. The woman at the bookstore also told me to visit a nearby naturopath. When he explained that parts of the experiences sounded like an out-of-body experience, I was once more shocked. I still was not sure what was going on, but I was relieved to know that these experiences were not as unique as I feared. I took the advice of the naturopath, and began to keep a journal.

Over time, I developed a good understanding of the psychic experience. It took a long time before I was comfortable with that word: "psychic". It seemed to go against everything I took for granted about myself. It was one thing to pick up the thoughts and emotions of my friends or a lover. It was quite another to be picking up on the feelings and experiences of total strangers.

There are many silly supermarket tabloid psychic predictions about celebrities. When I began to "tune in" to such people, I found the experience to be particularly distressing and disturbing, to put it mildly. It took years, but I finally found ways to "tune out" most of these unwanted messages.

Finally, I became so comfortable with my gifts that I was able to take a booth in a local "new-age" fair. There is nothing like the energy of thirty to a hundred psychics, all together in one room, to get the adrenaline going. There is also no other place in which you will find your "competitors" so willing to help teach, support and aid you through difficult times. Much of what I know now comes from psychics at these fairs. The fairs can also be stressful though. Overhead is considerable, and making a small profit demands you perform 30-60 readings in a three day period. I had not mastered psychic protection. It did not take long to get burned out.

I believe that the human nervous system functions as an "antennae" for psychic ability, and that certain areas of the planet are more conducive to psychic energy. And Vancouver BC (Canada) is one such area. Working in psychic fairs in Vancouver was beginning to wear on my health and well being. I decided to move to Toronto in an effort to find a more grounded and stable place to live. For the next eight years, I worked in the fledgling Internet service industry, taking only small numbers of readings and building a body of work on the World Wide Web in my spare time.

Then the "tech bubble" burst.

Unlike many others I was not surprised, I had actually seen this coming, but I was at a loss as to what step to take next with my life, and I realized that living in a large city like Toronto meant I was still absorbing emotions from the people in my community.

That was brought home to me with a shock when I took a short trip up into the Bruce Peninsula for a couple days. While hiking the Bruce Trail, I realized that I was totally alone, but I did not feel lonely – for the first time in months. I was absorbing the aggregate feelings of my stressed-out suburban neighbors. I sat down and had a good long cry, and decided then and there I was going to move out of the city.

Living With Your Psychic Gifts

Eventually I moved to a small town outside of Niagara Falls, which has been a huge help in bringing my abilities under control (In fact, I highly recommend country or small-town living to any hyper-sensitive psychic). I now prefer instead to teach others to learn to live with and use their gifts, rather than working directly with my own. Working full time as a professional psychic was only making my hyper-sensitivity that much worse.

Chapter Two
Am I Crazy? Or am I Just Showing Signs of a Psychic Gift?

This is the most frequent question I am asked. People who are having psychic experiences often come from family backgrounds where psychic experiences are portrayed as evil, taboo, or plain silly. When someone from such a background is in the middle of an unexpected psychic event, they don't question the wisdom of their family members or their cultural assumptions, they don't question the evidence, they first question their own grip on reality.

I regularly come across people who are showing signs of a spontaneous psychic awakening. Many of the events they describe seem mundane, amusing anecdotes to entertain friends at the campfire or dinner table. Much is made in the tabloid press of colorful stories of "deja-vu" or premonitions that seem to come true, but little is said about just how one goes about coping with an ongoing and unstoppable experience that can alter one's life. I myself went from one treatment to another, one book to another, one doctor to another, trying to figure out what was "wrong".

Living With Your Psychic Gifts

It was not until a naturopath suggested that my troubles stemmed from partial out of body experiences that I began to take my psychic side seriously. Before then, I dutifully consumed the anti-depressants my doctor gave me, and tried to ignore the impressions, visions and dreams. It was something like trying to sweep back the tide with a broom. My sense of depression and anxiety deepened, until I came to grips with the fact that I was psychic.

I now know that I am not alone. Many people struggle with this odd "gift", some aware, some not, that the trouble lies in accepting and using a psychic talent. The same energy that I once experienced as frightening now intrigues and exhilarates me. It is interesting and exciting to feel this energy move. It's heartwarming to watch people's eyes light up when I pass along a greeting from a loved one on the other side.

I believe that "psychic", "Chi" or "Kundalini" energy is the life force itself, and that all reality is simply a variation of the vibration rate of this energy, fundamentally a feature of the electromagnetic spectrum. It is only when this energy is blocked or misunderstood that we experience it as frightening.

Unfortunately, most people are barely aware of the blockages in their physical bodies, never mind of the blocks in their psychic bodies. On the rare occasion that they are confronted with a psychic event, they react with fear, because they do not understand what is happening.

There is a taboo in our culture about psychic gifts. Our minds are filled with inaccurate but popular media stereotypes of the "supernatural" and "occult". Psychic insight is often associated in popular media with madness. The person may fear being seen as "weird" or different. The only information available in the popular media is filled with stereotypes of the gypsy, witch and lunatic. Not the friendliest atmosphere to promote understanding! It is no wonder that people are in real emotional, mental and physical distress by the time they realize what the problem really is.

Some people are eager to pursue the gift, but are suffering from the misinformation, even, dare I say, quackery, of the books and information that are available. A lot of outrageous claims are made by those selling books and seminars, and it can be a challenge to sort through them, especially if your budget is limited.

There are good books available, but one must quickly learn to read between the lines, and to sort out the valid information from re-hashed "occult" nonsense. Those books which do not fall into the "pop-culture" category seem to be written for pseudo-scholars, to fill pages with huge volumes of bombastic prose in a misguided effort to appear more "scientific" or authoritative.

I will not make a claim to scientific method or "proof". I'm not qualified. What I believe comes through personal experience, mine, and those of clients, friends and peers.

In my opinion, the use of the psychic gift is an art, not a science. I feel the same may be said for any branch of psychology or medicine (at least as it is actually practiced, but that topic could be a book of its own). Even astrologers require an intuitive gift to be effective (though many claim this is not the case). All too often, fantastic claims are made for a certain book or treatment, and all too often they fail to deliver their promise.

If you do the exercises in *Living With Your Psychic Gifts*, you may begin to feel a lot calmer, find a sense of peace, and start to feel healthier. It may also be that you experience no changes whatsoever. In that case, the likelihood is that you will find a solution elsewhere, if you keep trying. This book, like any book on the subject, represents one person's subjective opinions, experience and research, and there are other methods and ideas that may be equally valid for you.

I remember a talk show where three different health experts were all insisting that his treatment was "the only" way to cure a certain disease. Each produced his scientific papers, his anecdotes, and a client cured by his method. Yet, one doctor was advocating macrobiotics, one, mega doses of vitamins, and one, a high fat, red meat diet! And throughout it all, each of these pompous, silly "scientists" maintained that the only way to treat the illness was by his method! It was sadly funny to the audience, who were aware that each method worked for different people with different needs.

Too many "new-age" metaphysical books fall into the same trap, claiming exclusive knowledge or information. While some of these books do indeed contain truth, many of them simply copy previously published sources. Such books are easy to spot.

Avoid any book that makes wild claims, or looks like a paperback version of a supermarket tabloid. Be skeptical of broad generalizations: "Anyone Can Astral Project in 80 Days" "Answers/Solves all Your Problems!" Put everything through your common sense filters.

If a book or teacher makes claims that seem too good to be true, then they probably are.

So ... *do* you have a psychic gift?

I believe that the energy I experienced as headaches and nightmares is the energy I now feel is healing and beneficial. It is the energy that makes psychic readings possible. Everyone who is alive makes use of this energy, because it is the fundamental life force itself. In the Eastern traditions, it is called "Kundalini". In the West we call it "psychic energy" or "vibes". George Lucas' concept of "The Force" is probably one of the best (though exaggerated) descriptions of this energy in modern fiction.

The mythology that surrounds the psychic energy can be confusing to the person who is just beginning to learn about their gifts. There are many different books written about this energy, but few of them are directed towards the Western mind set.

In the West it seems we are learning about this force almost from scratch. The symptoms of a psychic awakening can vary greatly, but they often follow a general pattern. Any person who has been meditating, praying regularly, or experimenting with altered states of consciousness leaves him/herself open to a

Kundalini or psychic energy experience. A few people, like myself, have not been consciously experimenting with psychic phenomena but may simply be close to someone who has. Psychic gifts can develop spontaneously. Since we are not exposed to many examples of this experience, fear begins to set in, and the person may try to cut off the flow of psychic energy. The genie can't be put back in the bottle, however. You can't quit a new reality like you quit a job. The more you try to hold back, the more insistent the energy becomes, until it can no longer be ignored.

The experiences sometimes take on a frightening aspect at this point. Because the person is fearful, they draw upon negative "vibrations" and their subconscious biases create visions of disasters or nightmares. Some psychics experience "Free Floating Anxiety" as one of my doctors called it. They are simply anxious, and they don't know why. There may be headaches, flashes of heat and vibrating sensations in the body. Some may "hear" voices, like whispers of memory. Still others see visions, or flashes of color surrounding people, and may be confused and frightened. Family and friends are rarely supportive, and the experience becomes more and more frightening until they subconsciously block the flow of energy altogether. For a time, life seems to go back to normal. But it soon becomes apparent that something is wrong. There may be bouts of depression. They become indecisive, and there is difficulty in concentrating. Memory problems can occur. In extreme cases, health, relationships and careers can be affected. The spectrum may run from a mild case of depression, to those where a person feels in danger of losing his or her sanity.

***When such symptoms are severe,
see your doctor.***

This is not just a disclaimer! The symptoms of psychic awakening are very similar to many illnesses, emotional, mental, and purely physical, and only a qualified physician can rule them out. You may discover that in fact, you do have a mental illness, but that does not mean your experiences are any less real. If you see a doctor, and get told that there is nothing mentally or physically wrong, only then you may be justified in concluding that the problem may lie with misdirected psychic energy.

The following list describes common signs of psychic energy. If you relate to the majority of these symptoms, and your doctor can find nothing wrong, then it is possible that you have psychic ability.

Signs of Psychic Energy

• Anxiety. "Free Floating" anxiety, when there seems to be no real reason to be anxious. Anxiety that hits in public places, old buildings or hospitals, but is not related to a fear that can be named.
• Emotional confusion. Emotions that are not related to current life events. You may feel sad, happy, enthusiastic or unmotivated for no reason you can name. At times, you may be able to connect these emotions to other people in the area.
• Vibrating sensations. From shaking hands to a sensation much like an electric shock. One of my clients described it like "An earthquake that only I could feel."
• Roaring noises in the ears.
• Poor concentration.
• Poor short term memory.
• Changes in energy level, too low or too high.
• Mood swings.
• Blackouts. A severe form of short-term memory loss. It is possible that you may be unconsciously "channeling".
• Small colored spots before the eyes. Often gray, blue or white, but can be any color. See an optometrist to rule out any physical causes.
• Vivid or lucid dreams.

Living With Your Psychic Gifts

- Precognition. Sensing events before they occur.
- Visions or hallucinations. Visions are much like memory images. Hallucinations seem real, but the person seeing them may or may not realize that they are not physical.
- Tingling or headaches in a band around the head.
- Sensing or seeing colors or auras, like flame surrounding people.
- Out-of-Body experiences. Seeing the body from a distance, floating above the body in a non-dream state.
- A new interest in the "new-age" or "occult".
- Struggling with "fate" and feeling like everything is going wrong all at once may indicate blocked psychic energy.

There is a special category of psychic that is near and dear to my heart. These are what I often call "suffering psychics" or "hyper-sensitives". These people are so psychic or empathic that they cannot block out the impressions, emotions or visions.

Remember that any and all of these symptoms may be caused by illness, drug/alcohol use, or by emotional or psychological disorders.

Caffeine opens the aura, making one vulnerable to anxiety attacks. Nicotine is grounding, which is why it is so calming, but it leaves a strong imprint on your energy (I know many good psychics who smoke and drink to excess). Alcohol is a major cause of both spontaneous psychic experiences and spiritual obsession. If you are suffering from over sensitivity, avoid alcohol altogether. Only once you have eliminated all medical, dietary, behavior and psychological possibilities, may you reasonably conclude that the only problem is that you are misdirecting psychic energy. These kinds of problems do frequently go together, however. After all, what happens on the psychic level is frequently reflected on the physical.

Never go off medication on the advice of a psychic or alternative medical practitioner alone.

Unfortunately, there is no standard of professional practice and many so-called "alternative health practitioners" are selling hope, not cures. Some are more effective than others, and no one treatment works for everyone. When in doubt, always consult a certified naturopath or herbalist. Always discuss alternative treatment with your doctor – some herbs and medications can interact badly.

Remember that many medications can be dangerous to quit "cold turkey". It is best to continue with a doctor's advice, while at the same time adding alternative practices such as meditation, natural herbs and vitamins, and sessions with healers and psychics. A professional alternative therapist will work with your doctor, and will never suggest you go off any medications or treatments without consulting your physician. If you can't be honest with your doctor, consider the possibility that you have the wrong doctor.

Am I crazy, or am I psychic?

Some mental illnesses, in my admittedly "layperson" opinion, are in fact causes for psychic experiences and vice-versa. Don't be afraid to admit you may suffer from depression, schizophrenia or other mental illnesses. There is no stigma attached to admitting you are ill unless you carry that judgment of others with similar challenges. What you have experienced as a hyper-sensitive cannot help but affect your well being. Mental illness is not a sign of moral or mental weakness. In fact, denying it could be the bigger weakness, because you deny yourself resources and information that could greatly improve, even save your life.

Living With Your Psychic Gifts

If you are given a diagnosis of schizophrenia or another mental illness, it may mean that some of your experiences are inventions of your own subconscious, and thus are not "real" according to objective standards. That seems to be a hard barrier to pass for some people who do suffer from legitimate mental illnesses. They don't want to be told that they are imagining things.

The truth is that healthy people "imagine things" too. I consider myself quite sane, yet, going back to my journals, I discovered that some of the events I recalled with perfect clarity were totally different than the events as I recorded them at the time! It was a huge shock to me to realize this at first. But it did not make me question my sanity or judgment. It merely made me more determined to keep good records of important experiences so I could learn more from them. I did not throw out all of my experiences because a few of them did not make sense. I realized that I was only psychic, not omniscient. Even the clearest psychics I know occasionally have moments where they are tricked by their own biases, desires or beliefs.

The main difference, perhaps the only difference, between the mentally ill psychic person and the sane one is in the level of comfort with which they approach a given situation. Depression, compulsions, anxiety, excessive amounts of fear, paranoia, obsessions, delusional thinking and physical discomfort can all be signs that you need help from a doctor or psychiatrist. Seeking such help is an affirmation of strength and character. You don't have to give up your beliefs or your connection to the world of spirit in order to get well and live a normal life.

So how do I tell the difference between something psychic and a fantasy? It can be very difficult to tell the difference - and there are actually four possibilities.

• It is "real" - in other words a valid psychic message, coming from outside.
• It is "unreal" - a valid psychic message, coming from outside, but coming from a spirit or source that is not trustworthy.
• It is "fantasy/wishful thinking/fear" - something that comes from the inner self.
• It is "mental illness" - a chemical or emotional affect of the mind.

Let's start with mental illness. The most well known sign of mental illness are messages that sound real - like voices that come from outside the head when no one else is around.

Psychic "voices" usually come across more like memories of voices, they are not usually actually audible (though some rare psychics do experience them this way). If the voice has an actual "sound" it may be an indicator of mental illness. Such voices are usually loud, insistent, demanding or derogatory. It's a painful, unpleasant experience. There is a lot of negative emotion related to it.

Of the others, there is no sure way to tell the difference except in retrospect. Once the information is checked against the results or against the facts, you'll know if the source was legitimate. I recommend journal-keeping over a long period of time - that is the only way to develop the intuition to know which "voice" is likely real, and which part is a reflection of the mind. The Oracle at Delphi exhorted "Know Thyself" - she was talking about this process. After 30 years I know where my blind spots are, and I still trip over them fairly often.

What are the different kinds of psychics?

There are a number of different types of psychics. Each kind is defined primarily by its analog in the physical senses. It is common for a gifted psychic to have more than one talent, but there is usually a primary gift.

Empaths are the most common psychics. They sense through emotions and feelings. Like "Counselor Troi" in Star Trek, they don't always have clear visions, but instead learn to interpret emotions in order to analyze events.

Clairsentient is another term frequently applied to empaths. A clairsentient "just knows things" and can't always tell you how.

Clairvoyants (literally "clear vision") primarily sense through dreams and visions. They will get a mental picture that is usually like a vivid daydream or memory.

Clairaudients get psychic impressions in the form of sounds or voices.

Precognitives sense the future in dreams or waking visions. This is usually a specific form of clairvoyance, though empaths can "project forward" with emotion to postulate a predicted outcome.

Psychometrists have the ability to sense thoughts, feelings and to relive events by handling personal items (usually jewelry) or by touching other people. This is a form of clairsentience that depends on touch.

Telepaths are the "mind readers", tuning into mental vibrations the way empaths use emotions. True telepaths are extremely rare.

Mediums are sensitive to ghosts, spirits and angelic guides. Mediums are often also empaths.

Channels, like mediums, are sensitive to spirits, but they may allow a spirit or guide temporary access to their own senses in order to facilitate direct communication. A "Conscious Channel" will remain control of all faculties during the experience and has full recollection. An "Unconscious Channel" may black out and have no recollections.

Living With Your Psychic Gifts

Hyper-Sensitives can be any kind of psychic, but the problem for them is that they cannot seem to shut off their abilities even when the information they get is confusing, painful or overwhelming. They tend to be empaths but may have additional abilities such as mediumship or clairsentience.

There are occasionally "psychic smells" or "ghostly touches", but there isn't a separate category for such sensations as they generally are not a primary talent. All the physical senses have psychic equivalents.

Psychic Attachments

There is another common kind of psychic experience, what I call "psychic attachment", where "meaning" becomes all-powerful. Quite often, psychics will become psychically attached to others. Sometimes this is a person they know, but it becomes overwhelming when it is a powerful, famous person, or someone in the public arena. Rock musicians for some reason seem to pop up a lot in attachment cases.

If you feel you have a psychic connection to a famous person, be extremely careful with your thinking. These kinds of connections can and often do become obsessive, and I believe some stalkers may be suffering from this problem.

Celebrity attachments are almost always unhealthy. If you pick up bits and pieces and there is no emotional charge, that's one thing. But often in attachment cases, the psychic begins to believe that the other party is aware of the connection, and that the connection is meaningful beyond a simple psychic exchange of information. That belief can become a powerful and unhealthy delusion.

Just because you have a psychic connection to someone does not mean you are destined to be romantic "soul mates". That is the most common assumption about this kind of experience. There is no certainty you will ever meet. You may never understand why this happened. As you grow, you'll find you have many powerful psychic connections to people you both love and despise, and even sometimes to non-human creatures, such as pets, and even to places. Enemies seem to be able to read each other's minds at times. True "soul mate" relationships are often among the most difficult, challenging, and often dysfunctional kinds of relationships, because they are meant to bring together two people who have issues to resolve.

The psychic part of the attachment itself is neutral. It has no innate meaning other than it exists. You choose what you think it means. There may be (incredibly rare) cases of attachments of this kind resulting in some kind of relationship, but I have never heard of any, and you are better off taking a doubtful approach to them.

So why does a psychic attachment so often lead to romantic delusions? I've seen a number of such cases, I experienced this myself, and in each case (including mine), the psychic was a poor, unknown, struggling creative person and the attachment was a form of escape from their ordinary lives. It sounds very harsh to drop the hammer on people's dreams, but that's all this is: a fantasy. Choosing to opt out of such attachments is the only sure way to ensure your emotional wellness. I have seen psychic attachment lead to serious mental illness. I believe some celebrity stalkers may also suffer from psychic attachments. Don't let this happen to you!

But <u>why</u> did this happen to me?

If you experience a psychic attachment or have a vision of an impending disaster, don't obsess over finding out "why". That will make you crazy faster than anything else you can do (I speak from experience). There may be no "why", at least none you may get to know in this lifetime. Sometimes things happen for reasons we don't understand, and that's okay.

I have yet to see even one ordinary friendship arise from an attachment case and I have never known of a plane crash or disaster diverted by precognition. I don't doubt this is (remotely) *possible*, but it isn't likely, and in most cases, assuming that is unhealthy. These things just happen, and maybe they are a kind of cosmic accident with no innate meaning. At best, they serve as wake-up calls to get us past our denial of our gifts.

Living With Your Psychic Gifts

If you experience a psychic attachment or have a vision of an impending disaster, and want to stop the connection, the best way is to mentally change the subject. Avoid listening to media reports about the person, avoid their music, art or films. Find something to do that will take your mind off them. Read Chapter Three, and perform the "Uncording" and other psychic protection procedures. Remind yourself regularly that the other party has no idea that anything like this is going on.

Chapter Three
Psychic Protection & Meditation Tips

One of my most common frustrations, from the days I worked in the psychic fairs, to current experiences in Internet mailing lists, is the amount of denial on the part of those I refer to as the "Purple Ladies".

We all know at least one "Purple Lady". She likes to dress in purple and even does her hair with purple highlights. Her home, office or booth is often filled with purple fairies and angels, and her response to every ill, real or imagined, is to "Be positive!" Negative things do not exist. Bad things can't happen if you are not afraid, if you stay positive.

Don't get me wrong. I like purple, fairies and unicorns too. I also believe it is vital to stay positive whenever possible. But unfortunately, bad things can and do happen, despite our best intentions. We cannot always control that. What we can control is how we *react* to these things. The Purple Lady is right that fear is one of the worst problems people face on the psychic plane. Our own fears magnify and intensify the experience, and can even twist a simply unpleasant encounter or inconvenience into a tragedy of seemingly monstrous proportions.

But the reality is that bad things can and do happen in the real world. It is prudent to be aware of those things, and to take action to protect yourself. In Chapter Thirteen, I talk about personal growth classes and how they can affect your well-being, not just psychically, but in every area of life. I have come to believe that self-awareness is the key to psychic health, and that psychic protection tends to be a bit of a crutch, however, these exercises still have a great deal of benefit, especially in times of crisis. They are a vital first step on the path.

The most important thing to remember is that fear itself is your worst enemy. I have been working with psychic abilities for over 30 years, and I have yet to encounter anything that could harm someone physically. Spiritual entities can scare you, they can be unpleasant, some will lie and deceive, but unless you give them power over you, they can't be much more than an inconvenience at times.

Yes, I have heard some horror stories, but they usually come from people with a particular religious axe to grind. You have to consider the source. You generally don't seem to encounter such beings unless you go looking for them, which makes me suspect that entirely human psychological processes are at work behind the scenes in the vast majority of these cases. I have found in my own experiences that overcoming my own fears and facing them directly was what actually resolved the problem.

Grounding

Grounding is the simplest and most often overlooked psychic exercise. Grounding is the process of re-connecting psychically to the earth or the ground, so excess energy can be diffused. The psychic grounding process is a close equivalent to the electrical grounding process.

If you are able to get outside, simply sit or bend down (remember to bend your knees) and touch bare earth. If you cannot sit or bend down, stand barefoot on the earth if you can. Occasionally you will feel an actual discharge of energy or a feeling of release. If you wish, you can imagine or visualize a cord of energy traveling from the centre of your body to the centre of the earth. This can also work if you cannot get outside.

One of the main symptoms of being ungrounded is feeling "scattered". You may also feel dizzy or anxious, and in extreme cases, you may feel electrical sensations in the arms or torso. If you feel such sensations, immediately dip your hands and feet in cold water.

If you find you suffer from being ungrounded a lot of the time, you may be a hyper-sensitive. It is a good idea for hyper-sensitives to avoid alcohol, tobacco, drugs and vegan diets. A small amount of meat and large amounts of legumes are good for grounding. If you feel you are ungrounded, avoid clear quartz crystals: wear onyx or hematite instead.

Keep in mind: it may take weeks of consistent grounding before you begin to feel better, especially if you are particularly sensitive. Any psychic work you do, any emotional trauma you experience will make you feel ungrounded again. This practice is something you must make part of your lifestyle. There is no "quick fix" for the sensitive. You will need to keep grounding to stay grounded.

White Light Exercises

There are a number of variations of this exercise, each more or less tailored to a particular belief system. The simplest version is to bring up the image of a blazing white light and surround your body with it, up to arm's length around you. You can "shower" yourself in it, or "cocoon" yourself, and it is best to practice with it on a daily basis so that you can bring it quickly to mind whenever you feel anxious or threatened.

Some may find this exercise to be overly energizing. Blue light works equally well, and I have found that golden sparkles in the image, or a "champagne" color works better. Experiment until you find the color that works best for you.

Stopping Deliberate Psychic Attacks

Deliberate attacks are extremely rare, but on occasion they do happen. You run across someone who is just plain manipulative, controlling and domineering. Suddenly you find out this person is "into" all kinds of scary things, and you notice you are run down, tired, suffer unexplained headaches, you have nightmares, and have a run of bad luck. It's possible you are under psychic attack.

I say *possible* because most cases of so-called psychic attack are really nothing more than emotions firing out of control, which is understandable when you run into a scary person who hits all your hot buttons. Even when there is a psychic component to the experience, the "attacker" is usually not aware consciously of the damage they have caused. I had this happen once when a well-meaning loved one was actually praying for me. This person was projecting their own fears into the prayer without realizing what they were doing. Regardless of whether or not it is a real, deliberate psychic attack, or you are just projecting your own fears onto someone else, the following techniques will bring back a sense of control and centeredness to you, and if you are under actual psychic attack, they should repel the attackers.

First, go out and buy a large quantity of pure rock salt and sprinkle it around your home. If you live in a house, bury salt in mason or glass jars at each corner of the property where the salt won't kill plants and will not be disturbed. Then going clockwise, draw a line of salt around the property (if this is not practical, you can do this as a visualization). Affirm to yourself that the purity of the salt will keep out all impure intentions, energies, spirits or people, and only allow beings and energies of good will to enter. Visualize a stream of white or golden light following you until it encircles your home. Feel free to pray for protection from anyone who may mean you harm while you do this - but ***not the suspected attacker specifically***. Remember that you may not be right about the source of your discomfort.

Next, buy some bay leaves, and tuck them under the furniture. If you live in an apartment, you can put the salt in small glass jars in the corners, and behind your furniture. You may also make or purchase "orgone" generators. These are devices made from resin, metal shavings and crystals. You can find sellers and how-to instructions online. You want to get generators with earth crystals in them, such as onyx, hematite, or smoky quartz crystal. Avoid clear crystals.

If anyone asks about the salt or generators, just say you heard that this generates positive energy and you are giving it a try - tell no one you are doing this for psychic protection, not even your loved ones. The reason for this is if it gets back to the attacker, he or she may push harder to get through. Skeptical friends and loved ones could leave negative thoughts behind that decrease the effectiveness of the process, or drag you down if they are not supportive.

Next, you need to go into a daily routine that will block and drive the "attacker" from your life. First is the realization that not everything bad happening to you necessarily comes from this person. *It doesn't matter whether they do or not because your program is designed to protect you from **anyone** or **anything** that may mean or cause you harm.* Do your best not to even think of this person. Whenever they come into your mind, think of something totally removed from them. Gently take your attention away from them onto something else. Do not allow yourself to dwell on them.

If you can, think of a place in your childhood or a scene from nature where you felt safe and happy. See yourself there surrounded by angels where they can't touch you. Or simply visualize a big red circle with a line through it over their face, and fade the image to gray in your mind. Then make yourself busy or distract yourself with other things until the thought passes. Don't get discouraged if this isn't easy at first. It's like exercising a muscle. The more you do it, the easier it will get. And don't be hard on yourself.

Don't let anyone tell you they can take care of a psychic attack or a "curse" for you for large sums of money. These folks are frauds and cheats by definition. Even if they were legitimately powerful psychics, all you'd be doing is trading one slave-master for another. You have the power within you to reclaim your life – no one else can do that for you.

Love Bombing

This is the simplest, safest, and most effective response to a deliberate or accidental psychic attack, especially when you don't know where it is coming from.

Meditate, relax, and focus your attention around your body. See if you sense any cords or attachments and mentally unhook them, sending them lovingly back to their source of origin. Send along pink, gold, or white light with the most positive, loving feelings that you can bring to mind.

Think of people and things that raise a loving feeling inside, and when you feel you have enough energy, push that loving energy in the direction of anyone who may wish you harm. Meditate on the loving feelings until you feel there is a "click" or a feeling of closure.

I believe Love Bombing is what is really meant by the challenge to "love thy enemies" in the Bible. It has never failed to have an immediately positive effect, and sometimes the results can be quite remarkable.

In some cases you may find former enemies turning into friends, in others, a persistent challenger simply backs off and disappears. On two occasions where I did this, someone I thought was a friend suddenly turned on me, then disappeared from my life. I immediately realized we were both much better off.

The best part about this meditation is it almost always works - even when you don't know who is behind the attack! And there is no "karmic payback". Some ritual methods, such as binding or taking revenge, can come back to you with unwanted and extremely unpleasant effects.

Blessed Candles

If you feel you are under attack and want a stronger focus, you can always add some blessed candles to your meditations. Get some good-quality candles from any source. Lay them in a plastic container filled with coarse salt for a few hours. Include some clear quartz crystals if you have them. You can expose them to sunlight (for a short period, remember they may melt), or the light of the full moon, pray over them, or hold your hands over them, visualizing white light pouring into them. Once they have been blessed, wrap them in a dark cloth, and put them away for future use. You can bless a variety of colors for specific purposes.

Cording

Cording is a form of psychic bond or attachment that binds two people together emotionally. Most cases of cording are accidental. Some are natural, and even helpful on occasion (when they happen with love and mutual consent). Most commonly, however, they are a symptom of a power struggle that can manifest as a dysfunctional or abusive relationship.

Clairvoyants can actually see these cords, and depending on their appearance, can tell two people a great deal about the relationship.

You don't need to be clairvoyant to release cords. All you need to do is visualize yourself and the person you think you've been corded to, and imagine that there is a string of energy connecting you. Make note in your journal of the exact place it is attached on both people. When you are ready, send a pulse of loving energy through the cord, then release or unhook yourself from it, and let it go. Sometimes you will feel a "snapping" sensation. Affirm that you are ready to release this person, and that all energy coming from them should be returned to them, with love, and for the greater good of all concerned.

Living With Your Psychic Gifts

It is important to keep in mind that you cannot harm someone by releasing a cord - nor does it mean that you must end the relationship. You can only cause harm if you attempt to uncord others without their permission.

Fretful parents who have a child involved in a corded relationship have on occasion approached me for help in "uncording" their child. I give them the same advice that I believe most skeptical non-believers would, "Keep your nose out of it until you are asked for help!"

If you attempt to intervene without permission from at least one side, it will come back to haunt you. I recall an email from one mother who did not listen to this advice. Her daughter is no longer speaking to her, and she has become the object of harassment from her daughter's former lover. I believe all she managed to do was move the cords from her daughter to herself. The bottom line is she violated a cardinal karmic law, she attempted to enforce her will over two others. She forgot that cords cannot form without consent from at least one side, and they cannot be dissolved without consent from at least one of the involved parties. She ended up doing the very thing she despised in others. That's not only hypocritical, it is plain wrong, regardless of one's motives - and it's dangerous.

Living With Your Psychic Gifts

If you can see a strong cord, but cannot tell your loved one about it in psychic terms, express your concern in more traditional ways. Tell them you are concerned that the other person is overwhelming or controlling them. Ask if you can pray for them. Visualization is a form of prayer. If they grant you permission to pray, ask for Divine Blessing before you proceed (according to your faith), and affirm that what you do be in accordance with Divine Will or is to be implemented in the higher good of all concerned.

Occasionally people will find it difficult to achieve a complete disconnection. This is almost always because they themselves at some level do not want to release the cord. Such attachments can be karmic, but they will always carry one of the following emotional charges:

Guilt. You may feel you have wronged the other party or acted badly and are secretly wishing you could make amends. You could be punishing yourself by clinging to the other person. Once you are able to forgive yourself, you may find that the cord releases on its own.

Anger/Resentment. Nelson Mandela once said "Resentment is like taking poison and hoping your enemy will die". This is one of the strongest things keeping people corded together.

It's also one of the most ironic. You wouldn't physically tie yourself to someone who abused you, but most people are out there emotionally bringing their abusers with them everywhere they go. When I first realized this I wanted to be sick, I realized I'd been dragging a bunch of bullies with me everywhere I went for 30 years. That made it much easier to forgive.

"Love-Desire". This kind of desire is really not love but is simply attachment. Attachment is what makes song-writers come up with such painful lines as "I can't live if living is without you". If the attachment is romantic, you want to be with the person, you want to make them want you too. It's painful to be away from them. If it's a friend or family member, you say you only want what's best for them, but really what you want is control.

"Love-Worry". Whether the relationship is romantic, friendly or familial, you have a different set of desires, values or beliefs, and want to control their behavior so they won't be hurt or you won't be hurt.

Tribal Bonding. Sometimes we fear letting go of an attachment because it strengthens our tribal identity. We all have many types of tribes, family tribes, friendship tribes, shared interest tribes, religious tribes. We may choose to stay attached to someone because of our family, work, social or recreational bonds. We may fear what others will think if we fully detach (as this may also mean ending a relationship).

Victim Bonding. The tribe in modern times with some of the strongest sticking power though is the "shared victimization tribe". A victim tribe can be healthy. It can start the road to healing. But it's meant to be temporary. As Carolyne Myss says, it's like a bridge to get you across a troubled patch of water. The problem is, many people are afraid to keep walking once they reach the other side. The victim tribe provides social connections, intimacy and identity ("I am a victim of ..."). It may provide power over others in social, family and work situations. Claiming victim status can get you out of work, end uncomfortable social situations, get you out of responsibility. I have even seen it used in discussion groups to end completely unrelated arguments. It can be pretty scary to let go of that kind of power over others. The problem is, it's got a hefty price tag: everywhere you go, you take your abuser along for the ride. Worse, you may drive loved ones away and create new abusers for yourself as other people react to your reactions.

Pride. Pride can come with tribal or victim bonding. A scary story can bring you lots of positive attention. If you are not getting positive attention in other ways, it can be easy to emotionally play up your attachment experience into a much bigger deal. The problem is, you end up perpetuating the attachment and empowering the other party as a result.

"Why". If I could erase one word in the English language it would probably be this word. One of the worst crazy-makers we have is this obsession we have with trying to figure out why something has happened to us. Imagine for a moment a fellow gets shot on the street corner. If he reacted to his physical wounds the way many of us do to emotional wounds, he would refuse treatment until he found out who shot him and why, and if he was like many of us, he wouldn't be happy until he also found out who made the gun, what bullets were used and why the owner of the gun shop got into the gun business! We have all known someone who takes their quest for answers from digging for insight to archeology, with no evidence they are overcoming their issues.

You may find that recognizing the reason you hang onto an attachment is enough to break its hold on you. If not, you may find a personal growth class could be helpful not just with psychic attachments but with your overall happiness in life.

If none of these seems to apply to your attachment, one good idea is to ground or center (See "Rainbow Meditation"), then allow yourself to feel the emotions you associate with the attachment. How do you feel about this person? What emotions come up in you as you think about the experiences you have shared? Is it okay for you to let them go? If not, why not? Explore those reactions and journal about them. That will give you some good clues what you need to do to let go fully.

Clearing

Do you feel like a human sponge? Ever notice that sometimes you absorb people's energies, and after a while you get so out of sorts you can't tell what emotions are really your own? You need to clear regularly, if you relate to that sensation.

I've found that there are four types of clearing rituals that are based on the elements. Whether or not they are effective depends on the elemental strengths and weaknesses of the psychic using them. To discover your elemental balance, visit www.astrology.ca and order a natal chart. It will give you a report that will tell you how many of your planets are in each element. If there is a strong imbalance, choose the clearing exercise that is suggested for the areas where you are weakest or strongest. Experimenting will show you which element works best for you.

Earth: Grounding exercises are the best clearing rituals for those of us with weak earth in our charts (this is common with empaths and hyper-sensitives, who are usually strong in Air and Water).

Water: The best way for low-water types to clear is to take a shower, and imagine that the water is washing away the excess emotion. If you can't get a literal shower, visualize a mountain stream or waterfall.

Air: Wind is your tool to blow away the emotions or energies - see them flying far away in your mind.

Fire: Light exercises are the safest tools for those with low fire energies. Imagine yourself surrounded in a glowing aura of golden light.

If you are not sure what your elements are, try each clearing exercise, until you find one that works for you.

Living With Your Psychic Gifts

Dealing with Fear

Do you remember the old saying "There is nothing to fear but fear itself"?

Since I first put the *Living With Your Psychic Gifts* site online I have received many letters from people who were relieved that they didn't have to fear their psychic experiences any longer. Sadly, I still get letters from people who continue to hold onto their fear.

Any unpleasant psychic experience has more power over you if you fear it. You may dislike the experience, it may be unpleasant, but ask yourself: aside from being frightened, have you come to any real harm? So, it can't really harm you, can it? I remember one scene from the movie "The Last Unicorn", where the Unicorn counsels the magician Shmendrik not to run from the attacking Harpy, saying "You must never run from anything immortal, it attracts their attention." Negative beings thrive on panic. The more upset you get, the stronger they seem to get. When you stop running, they lose interest (the same can be said for most human bullies).

You can't stop yourself from reacting fearfully at times. Some psychic experiences are disturbing and unpleasant. But holding onto your fear will not protect you from harm - it actually makes you more vulnerable. Don't "try not to be afraid" - that will be your first reaction, and you can't help that. You'll only end up beating yourself up for emotions that you can't control. What you can do is choose to release that fear. You can acknowledge your fear, then remind yourself that a psychic attack is just that - psychic. It can only harm you by causing fear. Once you remember that, the fear will pass much more quickly, and you will remember the techniques you've learned to drive out the negative energy. Eventually you won't react in fear at all.

I have been asked "What about evil spirits or even people who will not leave me alone?" Evil is an extremely strong word. I have met a few nasty, unhappy campers, but less than a handful of what I'd call truly evil beings (human, not discarnate). Nasty creatures (human or discarnate) may be confused, fearful, controlling or manipulative, but they are almost always operating from fear, not ill intentions. They do behave badly, and nobody wants them around ... but I wouldn't go so far as calling them evil. That kind of label only loads you both down with a lot of baggage, and makes them seem that much more scary and powerful than they really are. If you get a kick out of being scared (and some of us do, if we're honest), then keep this label "evil" for them. But if you truly want to move beyond these experiences, you will have to learn to forgive these beings, and even pity them, for they are truly stuck in patterns that you have chosen to outgrow.

Sealing Your Aura

Sealing your aura is extremely important especially after doing strenuous mental tasks. The effect of not sealing it is like leaving a big magnet out for various energies - and not all energies are necessarily good. There are many ways of accomplishing this, but my favorite is the one following below as it not only seals off your aura, but gives you a sense of protection.

Circle of Light

You can do the circle of light just about anywhere and it is simple and easy to learn. First, ground yourself. You must always ground before and after performing any psychic tasks. Now draw a circle around you in your mind. Imagine the circle bursting into a clear golden light. The light is loving, warm and protective. Pull the circle of light up. Watch it go over your head. Feel the warmth and love radiating from the wall of golden energy. Draw a protective symbol or imagine a blazing ball of energy above your head. Pull the positive energies in through your crown. Stop and feel the energy surging within the circle. Ground once more and feel protected.

Shields

There are many forms of shields. Shields aren't always effective. It's like wrapping yourself in a thick woolen blanket in the middle of a blizzard in a battlefield. It won't stop you from getting shot at, but it may help you feel warmer. You may find it a lot harder though to do battle!

Sometimes shielding can block out energy you do want as well. Others may feel this barrier and avoid you, when that was not your intent. You may also feel sluggish or confused if you are shielding too much. Shielding can be useful in emergencies, and it is good to practice when you are starting out, but don't worry about keeping it up as a daily practice.

Ground. Simply imagine some sort of substance around you. It could be in the form of a bubble or a wall. Another form is a thick bushel of leaves which people cannot see through. Tighten, reinforce, or even change the shield to a stronger material if you feel threatened. Use whatever symbolism fits for you. One of the best shields is an energy barrier that allows positive energies and intentions in, but blocks, bounces or returns any negativity to its point of origin. If you have trouble visualizing this, just set the intention as an affirmation: "This shield allows positive energies and intentions in, but blocks, bounces or returns any ill intentions, energies, beings or thought forms to their source."

Colors

Colors are incredibly important tools for psychics as they manifest in a variety of areas. They are often seen in auras, dreams and visions, and can have specific meaning, depending on the context. Each chakra or "energy wheel", the power centers in the body that meditation teachers associate with the endocrine glands, has a color association, and colors are often used in meditation and candle meditations to achieve specific effects.

Red: Anger, sexual energy, dynamic energy, fire, summer, life in its fullness, lust/passion, physical strength. You may see the color red in the aura in the area of the base of the spine, but when you see it in other areas, it can be an indication of high energy or injury. If you see it in dreams or visions, it may be an indication of anger or sexual energy. The more clear and strong it is, the more healthy it will be. Muddy or dark reds indicate injuries or upsets.

Orange: Sexual passion, healing energy. Orange in the body aura should be light, clear and strong, located near the sexual organs. In other areas, or in dreams and visions, it can indicate injuries in need of healing, or issues with sexuality, especially if it is dark or murky.

Yellow: Intellectual or rational energy, happiness, a youthful spirit, play, birth, beginnings, thoughts, ideas. If you see yellow in the aura, it is most likely to emanate from the Solar Plexus or lower chest area. When it is located around the head it can indicate great intelligence, strong ideas and a highly rational mindset. If dark or murky, it can indicate confusion or stressful thinking.

Green: Changes taking place, abundance, prosperity, hope, earth. Green is the "money color" in visions and dreams, and can show you areas of strong growth. The more clear and strong the color, the stronger the path to prosperity. If it is seen in the aura in the chest area, it indicates that the heart centre is strong and open. In other areas, it can show where the person is experiencing growth. Dark, muddy greenish-brown spots can be an indicator of cancer or other "over-growth" diseases.

Blue: Peacefulness, positive emotions, introspection, intuition. Blue is a calming, cooling, protective energy, which is often seen in the throat area of the aura. In the head region, it can indicate a person with strongly spiritual thoughts. Dark, muddy blues in the area of the throat can indicate someone who has a difficult time expressing himself or herself. It may indicate throat or thyroid problems.

Purple: Protective spiritual energies, higher intelligence, aspiration. Purple is one of the highest spiritual colors, but it can be over-used by those who are drawn to spiritual interests. We live in the real world and the ideal state of affairs is a fully balanced spectrum. But occasionally you see these people I call the "Purple Ladies". If you have ever met one, you know what I mean. This is someone whose home, hair and wardrobe is a variation of light shades of purple. Their eyes are often glassy, and their thoughts ... ephemeral. Dark strong purples, royal purples, indicate prosperity and power. Medium shades and lavenders indicate spiritual interests. Muddy, swirled colors could indicate spiritual confusion.

Indigo: Self-control, the Third Eye. It is rare that Indigo comes up in a dream or vision. When it does, pay attention, because your Third Eye or ability to foresee the future has been activated. A lot of indigo in an aura can be an indication of advanced spiritual development.

Violet: Spirituality. Violet is a shade of reddish-purple and its meaning is similar.

Pink: Peace, calmness. Pink is another protective color, and generally indicates a feminine, healing, nurturing energy. It is often seen at the top of the head in the aura. It is also being used in prisons and hospitals to encourage a peaceful, calming effect.

Silver or Grey: Grey usually indicates confusion, while silver is usually a color of an inner aura called the "Etheric Shield". Some psychics have also seen a "Silver Cord" that connects the soul to the body during out of body or near-death experiences. The Silver Cord is also mentioned in the Bible (Ecclesiastes. 12:6).

Gold: You will rarely see gold in the aura, but occasionally when you encounter very high spiritual frequencies, you may see it around the top of the head. It is important in protective visualizations, and is of course an indicator of prosperity in dreams or visions.

White: Purity and clarity. White is a combination of all the colors and is often recommended in protective visualizations. You may see white spots in the auras of some psychics whose auras are a little too open. If you see a lot of white spots in your own vision, and you don't have eye problems, your own aura may be a little too wide open. You may also be having spiritual or angelic visitations. It may also be seen in the top of the head or behind the eyes during powerful meditations.

Black: Transformation, mysteries, hidden things. Black in the aura is a strong indicator of illness or disease in the area of the body where it is seen. Black in visions and dreams indicates hidden things, mysteries, and can indicate illness or negative intentions.

Herbs and Psychic Growth

There are numerous herbal remedies that may be helpful to the psychic or sensitive. Before you try any herbal preparations, it may be a good idea to check with your doctor or a qualified herbalist. Herbs are powerful medicinally and while interactions and side-effects are rare, they do occur. If you are pregnant or may become pregnant DOUBLE CHECK with your doctor - some herbs can cause miscarriages.

The most common issue for sensitives is of course depression, and for mild cases of depression, Lavender, St. John's Wort and Kava Kava, Turmeric, and 5-HTP are often reported to be effective.

Another helpful treatment you can buy at most health food or new-age shops is Bach Flower Treatment's "Rescue Remedy" formula. If you are avoiding alcohol though, be aware it is mostly alcohol. Even 4 drops may be too much if you are 12-stepping.

Essential Oils

I prefer the essential oil version of most herbs. You may find that a lot of the so-called "essential oil" and "aromatherapy" oil products sold cheaply in drug stores and supermarkets are either cut with large amounts of carrier oils, or are entirely synthetic oils. It is okay to use them for scenting a potpourri jar, but they do not have medicinal effects, including the calming and healing effects most sensitives are looking for. The power is not in the fragrance alone - real essential oils are the "life blood" of the plant. Their molecular weight is small, so they easily penetrate the skin, quickly entering the blood stream, carrying their active ingredients directly where they are needed. The same is not true of synthetics and perfumes. If it does not say "pure essential oil" chances are good there are chemical additives and carrier oils present. You do get what you pay for in essential oils.

Real essential oils are powerful! Do not use them "neat" unless an aromatherapist tells you it is safe to do so. Do a small "skin test" to ensure you are not allergic, especially before using them in a bath. Avoid any contact with the eyes.

Here are some common herbal oils and their psychic/spiritual/healing uses. This is not an exhaustive list. I have tried to focus mainly on the most common herbs in use by psychics.

Birch: A good anti-inflammatory and respiratory herb, Birch is grounding and opens spiritual and creative channels.

Cedarwood: A good aid to meditation, calms aggressive or angry thoughts, grounding, anti-inflammatory. A good protective herb for those under psychic attack, or who have weakened auras. Cedarwood brings the body into balance.

Chamomile: Commonly used as a night-time tea and "blonde hair rinse", chamomile is a powerful anti-inflammatory oil. Good for insomnia, headaches, calming hypersensitivity, restlessness, depression, anger and fear. Avoid using during pregnancy.

Cinnamon: An oil long associated with prosperity, it is a powerful purifier, burning away negativity and confused thoughts.

Fennel: Protects against negative thoughts and may be helpful in warding off psychic attack. A beneficial side effect for cat-lovers: fleas can't stand fennel!

Jasmine: Relieves depression, lightens the mood, and may make your partner frisky as a side benefit! Cleanses the aura and brightens the emotions.

Juniper: Strengthens the nervous system, helps restore strength after stress. Do not use if pregnant or if you have kidney disorders.

Lavender: The queen of oils - a good all-purpose healer. If you are not sure which oil to use, try lavender. Calms but stimulates. 3 drops on a pillow assists in a good night sleep. Be aware that using too much lavender may keep you awake however. Lavender can be used undiluted on troubled skin. Naturally antiseptic and antibiotic, it also repels fleas and mosquitoes. 6-10 drops in bath to calm, ease fatigue and lower stress levels. 20 drops to 60 ml carrier oil for massage.

Marjoram: Calms, strengthens, and helps you confront personal issues. Is helpful in healing grief after loss. Calming to hyperactive people. Combine with Lavender and Peppermint to clear sinuses and combat headaches.

Mugwort: Calms, helps in meditation, but is mood altering, heightens psychic sensitivity, and may promote astral experiences. If you are too psychic, avoid this herb!

Patchouli: Opens the heart centre - is commonly used as a love or passion oil. May be used to attract a loving mate.

Peppermint: A good anti-anxiety herb, Peppermint also is good at fighting nausea and car-sickness. Mix half and half with lavender for use in calming migraines.

Rose: Rose oil is incredibly uplifting, being sacred to the goddess Venus - but it is also the most expensive of essential oils. Expect to pay over $150 dollars for a small bottle of the real essential oil.

Rosemary: Enlivens, energizes, strengthens the mind, enhances memory.

Sage: Sage is often used as an aid to meditation, to ease depression, and the dried herb is burned to purify the home of negativity and unwanted energies. Sage is calming and peaceful, and may enhance and clarify psychic impressions.

Sandalwood: Peace, acceptance, comfort for the dying. Sexual restorative. Soothing and hydrating for the skin. May help with acne.

Yarrow: Use to mend holes in the aura, to drive off energies that are not your own, to reclaim your psychic space if you have been abused or violated.

*Your experience may vary - these are personal observations and I am not a doctor, nor a trained aromatherapist. If you are pregnant or think you may be pregnant, check with a doctor and a trained aromatherapist before using any essential oil.

Crystals and Psychic Growth

Crystals have been used since pre-historic times for medicinal and magical purposes. Each different crystal comes with its own particular properties and associations. For the hyper-sensitive, avoid clear crystals and choose black, dark, or milky stones as they tend to have better grounding properties. Clear quartz should be avoided at all costs. Never under any circumstances should a hyper-sensitive have anything but a grounding crystal in the bedroom, and clear quartz should not be worn on the body, ever.

Agate: Strength, courage, perceptiveness. Grounding. Astrological Association: Gemini.

Amazonite: Aligns and balances the psychic and etheric bodies. Brings joy, peace, happiness and clarity. A "love" stone. Astrological Association: Virgo.

Amethyst: Peace, calmness, meditation, spiritual purity, Divine Love. Astrological Association: Pisces/Aquarius.

Aquamarine: Aids self-expression, calms the nerves, banishes phobias. Astrological Association: Pisces/Aquarius.

Citrine: A prosperity stone, citrine aids in raising and warming your spirits while it attracts higher energies. Astrological Association: Gemini/Aries/Leo.

Clear Quartz: Energy - pure, raw power, it should be avoided by hyper-sensitives as it amplifies thoughts and emotions, and heightens psychic sensitivity.

Fluorite: A "balancing" stone, this multi-colored stone promotes balance and intuition. Astrological Association: Pisces/Capricorn.

Hematite: The best stone for hyper-sensitives as it connects you to earth energies and grounds you while strengthening the physical and psychic bodies. Astrological Association: Aries/Cancer/Aquarius.

Malachite: Balances and clears emotions, clears subconscious blocks. Astrological Association: Cancer/Scorpio.

Rose Quartz: Calms, promotes loving feelings, clears anger, harmonizes and balances. Astrological Association: Taurus/Libra.

Tiger Eye: Balances energies, is somewhat grounding. Astrological Association: Capricorn.

Turquoise: Peace, understanding, enhances psychic energies more safely than clear quartz. Astrological Association: Sagittarius/Pisces/Scorpio.

Regardless of what other psychic protection techniques you are using, do the "White Light" visualization twice daily at morning and night as well, and "uncord" yourself often.

Living With Your Psychic Gifts

Chapter Four
Controlling Psychic Growth

Controlling psychic ability can be difficult. The accuracy of psychic impressions has been shown to change accuracy with the phases of the sun and moon, women's cycles, the geo-magnetic pull of the planet, physical location, and the emotional and physical state of the psychic. I personally found that the client's state of mind at the time of a reading makes a big difference in the quality of a reading. If my client was indifferent, then it was difficult for me to be clear as well. If they intended to stump me, I did often realize this quickly, but some psychopathic people, those without empathy or true emotions, would be able to fool me utterly. I would only pick up the false persona they were projecting. Such individuals are rare, however.

Some drugs alter consciousness, open the aura and make one more sensitive to psychic vibrations. I do not recommend that you experiment with drugs. I have never tried psychedelics, but have been told by others, and have read that they totally open you up to psychic abilities. One friend described experiences that were very similar to my own Kundalini or sleep-paralysis experiences after his experience with ayahuasca. There can be such a thing as "too much of a good thing"! Alcohol can be particularly dangerous, especially if you are already too sensitive. It leaves a psychic residue that lasts up to 24 hours or more.

Remember to raise white light when you enter any pub or bar, or when you visit anyone with a drinking problem. Bars are usually full of lower astral energies, and the emotional imprints of their clients. Tobacco is grounding, but its effects are temporary, and it leaves one more sensitive when it wears off. If you are having vibration sensations or anxiety attacks, I recommend that you abstain from street drugs, tobacco and alcohol completely.

Alcohol, strict vegetarian diets, celibacy and excessive mediation are also frequently behind over-sensitivity. You may want to experiment with dietary changes to see if you are also sensitive to certain foods. Fragrances can be triggers to sensitive people as well.

One thing that you must learn to do is to suspend judgment. Your own opinions, biases and background will come through in your intuitions. Psychics with Christian backgrounds may speak of "Christ Consciousness", those with an Eastern bias may speak of "Kundalini" or "Chi", yet each may be sensing the same force. The different terminology is simply a cultural affect. Each is describing it according to his or her understanding. As you develop your intuition, you will begin to discover your own biases, and hopefully overcome them.

Each individual is like a single facet in an incredibly complex crystal. Each reflects exactly the same energy, but the pattern may look different because of the shape or size of the facet. No two crystals will reflect the sunlight in exactly the same way, but this does not change the sunlight. Our goal is to bring through the light as clearly as we can, while recognizing our limits. The better we know ourselves, the clearer our intuitions will become.

Fate

Your beliefs about "fate" are another important component to understanding your psychic gifts. Those who do believe in fate must necessarily believe that there is no such thing as free will. If something is fated, whatever happens will happen, there is nothing you can do about it. You may meet a lot of these people in your travels – the Eastern cultures and philosophies tend to swing in that direction.

Living With Your Psychic Gifts

In the West, we tend to have a greater emphasis on individual will and freedom, thus our philosophy towards prediction is less fatalistic. As Yoda says in "Star Wars", the future is always in motion. There seems to be no point in knowing the future if you can't change it. What you will find as you journal is that upcoming energies are in fact fairly resistant to change. By becoming aware of those upcoming energies you can change how they manifest, however. You can choose how to react to them.

When the local weather forecaster predicts rain tomorrow, you can't change the fact that it will rain. But that does not mean you will necessarily get wet. You can stay at home, wear a raincoat, or carry an umbrella. Any of these choices could dramatically change your relative dampness, not to mention other events in the day (like your boss's mood if you show up soaking wet for an important meeting).

If you sense an upcoming disaster involving an automobile, you may choose to drive more carefully or have your car taken in for a safety check. It may still be a challenge if you find all your brake pads need replacing, but that's not the same thing as having to replace a totaled car. If you sense children coming into your life at a certain time, you can decide to have a child of your own, or monitor your birth control, but you may end up working with children or helping out a local school. The energy will find a way to manifest itself. By being conscious of it, you can often mold it in a more desirable direction.

Unfortunately there are times where there is nothing you can do to prevent a disaster you have foreseen. After 9-11 I got the most heartbreaking letters from people who felt helplessness, despair and guilt because they had foreseen this tragedy and there seemed to be nothing they could do to prevent it. I had foreseen parts of the tragedy myself, but could not pin down the place or time. I had even predicted war and disaster that week in my astrological column. In retrospect it all seemed so obvious! Why did each of us get one piece or the other, but not a cohesive picture? Why couldn't we have prevented this?

I don't know.

Why are we sometimes given visions of things we cannot change? My theory is that the human capacity for conscious use of the psychic gift is a relatively new development in our evolution, and these are random "accidents". Powerful emotional events do seem to leave "psychic scars" in space and time, in ways we don't fully understand. To take on personal responsibility for such global tragedies is a recipe for misery.

Living With Your Psychic Gifts

When you foresee a disaster there is often no way to warn people. I know of at least two psychics who volunteered information to police about a local murder case, and were arrested for the crime because it seemed to them that the psychic knew too much. The psychic was cleared in the end in both cases, but it was a hard lesson that our world is not quite ready for this kind of information.

If you have a vision like this, by all means take note of it, journal on it – share it in the online discussion group (There is a link on www.psychicprotection.net).

Remind yourself that you are probably not the only one seeing it, that there may be nothing you can do about it, and that it cannot harm or affect you. It's only a vision. Having a vision like this does not mean you have to act on it. Don't apply meaning to it that is not innate in the process. There is no "why". It is. It just is.

Journaling

Journals are the best way for you to keep one foot firmly planted on the ground while you are exploring your psychic abilities. If you take no other suggestion from *Living With Your Psychic Gifts*, at least start journaling regularly.

Faulty memories can interfere with a psychic's growth. It is easy to blow a situation out of proportion, or to diminish it when there is no objective record of events. One time I had a premonition come true, and one part of that premonition involved the presence of a bright green apple. When it finally happened, I ran back to my journal and was stunned to see I had written bright red apple instead! By the time the experience completed that one small detail was firm in my mind: green apple. But in the original premonition, I had actually written red. The reset of that premonition was entirely true to the original perception otherwise. You will be amazed to discover just how fickle and tricksey your memory can be when you need to recall old memories, especially dreams.

If you are keeping a journal and your visions have come true, then you will have a clear record of the experience. If not, then a journal will keep you from exaggerating a simple impression into an earth shaking drama. I often see people in distress who are suffering from wildly exaggerated memories of events their loved ones do not share. A journal can be a wonderful reality check.

You should record all impressions, no matter how vague or strange, especially when you are first starting out. Record all your dreams, especially the vivid, lucid "more than a dream" dreams. You may be surprised to discover that weaker impressions sometimes prove more accurate than deeply emotional visions. Try to record them all. Record impressions that come to you when you visualize or meditate. Keep track of your moods, and of major experiences in your life. If you are a woman, keep track of your cycles. Sometimes it is a good idea to find a partner, a friend to confide your experiences to. That way, you can have another point of view, and a witness to events as they unfold.

Remote Viewing

Many people are starting "psychic circles" to experiment with clairvoyance or remote viewing, and coaches such as myself offer workshops in different psychic arts. One of the tools we use in classes on psychic development is the remote viewing experiment. You can try this in groups, or one on one. One person draws or chooses an image at random. At first, this image is limited to geometric shapes or simple images. Later, it is expanded to include people, thoughts and emotions. The "sender" writes his image down in a journal, and concentrates on it.

The sender must try to clearly visualize the image. At the same time, the "receiver" creates the image of a blank screen in her mind. The receiver records all impressions in her own journal. When they are compared, you may find that there are many ways of sensing or seeing energy. Remote viewing is very good practice for developing control. It will help you to get the feedback and ideas of your partner. One may find that she or he describes things primarily in terms of ideas, the other in terms of emotions.

One gifted psychic I know often senses energy, and describes it in different ways from my interpretations. I might say, "It feels lonely, hollow and empty. It is round and hard." He would likely describe it as, "A round, hollow object." Eventually, we both realize we are describing a ping pong ball. Our perspectives work together well, and you may find that interaction with other, more experienced psychics is one of the best ways to begin to develop control over your psychic gifts.

Card-Guessing

You may buy "Zenner Cards" at some new-age bookstores. These are the famous cards some scientists used to test psychic ability in laboratory experiments. They contain five basic symbols, a square, circle, wavy lines, plus sign and triangle. You may also find Zenner games on the Internet.

I advise against using Zenner Cards as a technique to hone psychic abilities. It may be a fun game or distraction, but there is little if any benefit in it psychically. There may be a small indication of hits at the beginning of the test, but it quickly drops off over time. Skeptics say this disproves psychic ability. I say it proves boredom can affect results in psychic testing! Since most hyper-sensitives are empaths, and cards with printed symbols have no feelings, I am not surprised the results are not particularly compelling.

Living With Your Psychic Gifts

Meditation

It is vitally important to establish a regular meditation schedule, ideally once in the morning on awakening, and once just before bedtime. There are specific meditations outlined in *Living With Your Psychic Gifts*, and there are a number if links on the web site where you can purchase and download guided meditations. I highly recommend James Roswell Quinn's "Centering" CDs (www.lovebasedleader.com). You can use one of these, or one of your own, but the daily discipline will help calm and focus your mind, making your other exercises that much more effective.

Oracles – Tarot & Astrology

There are many valuable tools, called oracles, that a person can use to fine tune or develop psychic abilities. The Tarot is a complex deck of 78 cards, and is based on numerological, astrological and other ancient symbolism. "The Way of Cartouche" is a beautiful set of 25 Egyptian cards, especially designed with beginners in mind. The Runes are a set of 25 stones, each carved with Viking symbols. The Karma Cards, based on astrology, are simple and straightforward, needing almost no interpretation. There are many different sets on the market, each reflecting a different cultural background or set of interests. It is a good idea to study and experiment with different oracles before you choose one.

I now feel that Tarot primarily reflects fears and desires of the client, and sometimes the reader. It is not always right about objective reality. I find it most helpful as a tool for focusing on the present, or for asking what people fear or think, for studying symbolism, and less useful as a practical oracle for seeing the future.

The choice of a Tarot deck is a personal decision, but it is often influenced by the choice of cards your teacher or mentor uses. Many people start out with the Rider-Waite deck, as it is the most popular, well-known deck. Most books on interpreting Tarot use the Rider-Waite symbols as well, so finding a good book of interpretations is not difficult. Many people find this deck harsh, however, and soon move on to any of over thirty different decks before too long. A Tarot deck is a personal tool, and it should reflect your character and tastes. For those interested in learning about the Tarot in depth, there are two wonderful authors who have written extensively on the subject. Norma Cowie publishes her own books in Canada (www.normacowie.com). Nancy Garen's books simplify the Tarot, and make it easy for anyone to read the cards (www.nancygaren.com).

The best way to learn any system is to use it. You need not memorize all 78 cards. In fact, it may be best that you come to your own understanding of each card. That way, you will give more complex, personal readings when you read the Tarot. Start with one book of interpretations. You can throw away the little pamphlet that comes with the deck. It is far too simplistic to be useful in a real reading.

Draw your card or cards, then ask yourself, what does the symbol on this card say to me? What feelings does it bring up? The emotions that you feel are frequently more accurate than some interpretations "by the book". The best way to become familiar with an oracle is to draw a daily card and record it in an oracle journal. Choose a question that you will use every day. I usually ask, "What kind of day will I have today?" At the end of the day, compare your experiences to the meanings usually attached to the card. As your experiences grow, you will discover the unique pattern of interpretations that you will call your own.

Say you choose to use the Tarot. The card you draw is "The World". The first thing to notice is that "The World" is a picture of a woman, who dances, nearly naked, against a sky blue background. She is surrounded with a laurel wreath. The picture is framed by symbols of the four elements, the lion, angel, eagle and bull.

What do these symbols mean to you? If you have difficulty in interpreting symbols, put yourself in the place of the character represented in the card. Invent a story about her. How would you fell, if you could dance, naked in the clouds, with the symbols of abundance all around you? Would you feel special? Would you feel freedom? Or would you feel responsibility? Tell yourself a story about the woman in the card, and write it down. At the end of the day, compare the actual events of the day with the story you wrote down.

Don't be discouraged if there seems to be no correspondence at first. You are simply experimenting. You will need to develop your skills at interpretation, and this is an art, not a science. You may discover that your own interpretations seem to contradict those of the more established psychics. Don't be too concerned. Often times, the apparent contradictions disappear when an interpretation is re-examined from another angle, or is reworded slightly. Sometimes, strong cultural differences, or religious opinions can color interpretations too. If you feel confused about

Living With Your Psychic Gifts

the meaning of a card after you have studied it, you may wish to meditate on the symbol for a short while. Relax and study the card. Ask what message this card may have for you.

Once you feel confident in your psychic skills, you will no longer need to rely on an oracle to help you focus. This process may take days, weeks or months. Some excellent psychics never outgrow the need for the Tarot, or other, more complex tools like astrology or numerology tools. There is no timetable for growth. You don't need to become a professional to live with your psychic gift.

Some psychics I know say that one should not use the Tarot to do readings for oneself. I disagree. However, one must be careful to avoid self-deception. When you read for yourself, you cannot be truly objective. Keep a journal, and you will always have a record of exactly what you have sensed. The only way to get to know the Tarot or any other psychic tool is to use it. Many beginning psychics are reluctant to do readings on people around them, because they are not confident enough in their skills. Only you can know if or when you will be ready to do "readings" for other people. I do recommend against it as a career choice for most hyper-sensitives however, as repeated opening to psychic ability only increases your sensitivity.

Another misconception is that the Tarot cards actually control the future. I have known the cards to be wrong from time to time, and if they controlled the future, they could not be wrong. Tarot cards simply reflect the energy of the moment to the reader.

I prefer using astrology, not only for traditional readings but for personal growth and self-knowledge. Knowing your own chart is an excellent way to get started in astrology. There are a great many astrological resources online. Astrology is much more accurate at determining the timing of events, and it is frequently a more detailed source of information.

There is one caveat I would offer about astrology and that is, like any other metaphysical art, it's not always possible to determine how a given set of energies will manifest. In two people with the same chart, you may see Mars conjunct Venus. But one person will fall in love on that day, and another out of love. Another might start a new job they love. Other aspects within the chart may give hints, but you really need to know what else is taking place in that person's life before you can guess at how that energy will manifest. And you will be guessing! Astrology isn't always clear in advance, though it usually is in retrospect.

Channeling, Ouija & Automatic Writing

Many people have experimented with Ouija Boards, automatic writing and channeling - inviting spirits to enter their bodies in order to gain wisdom, insights or guidance. Some have had very positive experiences, and for others, these practices have led to disaster.

> *I advise all "hyper-sensitives" to*
> *avoid channeling, Ouija Boards*
> *and automatic writing.*

Other psychic teachers swear by these tools, but this book was developed with the hyper-sensitive in mind. If you do take a chance on opening yourself up through one of these tools, it is at your own risk. My belief is that these tools are not negative or evil in and of themselves. I believe that the negative cultural associations we have with them, and the fact that some of their proponents, and in Ouija's case, the manufacturer, treats them like a game. People don't realize that they are opening themselves up to all their emotional baggage by playing with these tools, and they are not ready when challenges occur.

Living With Your Psychic Gifts

Often, teachers of channeling and automatic writing fail to teach even the most basic grounding and psychic protection exercises, and that's the main reason I advise against these tools. I have heard of some negative experiences with Tarot as well. So if in doubt, leave them alone until you feel more grounded and secure.

Chapter Five
Dreams, OOBEs, Auras, the Etheric Body and the Astral Plane

After you start getting comfortable with your psychic experiences, you will start to hear some terms you have never heard before, like "the Astral Plane" and "Out Of Body Experience" or "OOBE". The average hyper-sensitive will have a number of these experiences, but may not have all of them. Psychic talents are like creative talents, one artist may focus on painting, another likes poetry. One psychic may have many astral experiences, another sees auras, while yet another only has the occasional vision from time to time.

Understanding these different processes though is important, because they can happen periodically without warning, and if you know to expect them, they won't seem frightening or unusual to you.

Dreams – Lucid, Precognitive Repeating and Shared

When you start to journal, it is important to keep track of your dreams, because you'll find that your psychic talent creeps into this area of your life more often than you realize at first. Most of these experiences will be symbolic rather than literal, but they can at times portend future events, and may be amazingly accurate reflections of your current state of health and well being.

Regardless of the type of dream experience you have, you can gain more control over it, and make it more valuable by keeping regular journals of your dreams. You can keep notes with a pad of paper and pencil, but if you are an active dreamer, you are also likely to be a light sleeper, and may find it hard to get back to sleep if you are up frequently transcribing your dreams. Many psychics also suffer from sleep disorders. A bedside tape recorder allows you to quickly note the dream and get back to bed. You can transcribe the dream to paper later. In fact, doing it this way will help you realize just how much recollection you are losing and what to watch out for.

If you snore heavily, suffer from insomnia, or your partner says you stop breathing in your sleep, get a referral to a sleep clinic. Sleep apnea is a common factor in many psychics. When I got a CPAP machine to assist with sleep apnea, one welcome side effect was an almost complete end to the frightening night-time vibrating paralysis experiences I was having.

If you think you don't dream, you may be a heavy sleeper, though I find this is rare among hyper-sensitives. Most of us have some kind of unusual sleep issue. You may be able to gain memories of dreams by setting your alarm an hour or two earlier than you normally wake, then writing down or taping anything you remember. As you practice, you'll find you are able to recall more and have more vibrant and interesting experiences.

Lucid Dreams

Sometimes when you are in the middle of a wild dream, things get so weird that it dawns on you that you are dreaming. Experienced lucid dreamers are as often as not aware and "awake" during dreams, able to direct events to greater or lesser degrees. It is my belief that during lucid dreams, the dreamer is at least partially entering the astral plane.

Directed Dreaming

Some lucid dreamers are able to consciously direct their dreams. They focus on a particular question or area of life before they go to bed, and ask for spiritual guidance, or guidance from their inner selves, and claim to be able to come up with amazing solutions in their dreams.

Shared Dreaming

It is rare, but it has been known to happen. Two particularly sensitive people may share the same dreams. I remember one case where I dreamed that I was on the seashore in Calgary Alberta – a landlocked prairie town. One of my roommates the next morning reported he had the same dream, and had waved at me from one of the boats. I had seen him and waved back at him.

Dream Symbols

Regardless of the type of dreams you have, there is likely to be at least some form of symbolic content. I won't get into specific symbols here, and have not provided a "dream dictionary" in *Living With Your Psychic Gifts*, because I don't believe in dream dictionaries. They are too rigid, and don't account for social, cultural or religious differences. While some symbols are universal (coins are almost always indicators of money), other symbols are not so ubiquitous. Snakes are a good example. In some cultures and religions, they are seen as symbols of spiritual wisdom. But many in our culture have phobias and see them as symbols of evil. The context of the dream can make a big difference in its interpretation.

When there is a symbol or series of symbols in a dream that you don't understand, talk it over with trusted friends. Ask them what it means to them. Ask yourself, what does this mean to me? What were my emotions during that part of the dream? What else did I remember or notice? Don't get hung up on one part of the dream. Remember what Freud is supposed to have said, "Sometimes a cigar is just a cigar."

OOBEs and NDEs

These odd acronyms stand for "Out Of Body Experiences" (OOBE) and "Near Death Experiences" (NDE). The NDE happens after a traumatic experience, where the person comes near to death, and in some cases, has been pronounced dead by doctors. When they are brought back to life by medical intervention, they report an amazingly consistent story of being pulled through a tunnel of light into a heaven-like place of pure love. Often they are met by loved ones or relatives, and sometimes even pets who have passed on before them. Often, they are given a choice whether or not to come back to life, but are sometimes told they must come back, that it is not their time.

This "heavenly place" is very similar to the place where some people go during Out of body experiences. In the OOBE, there is no physically traumatic experience, though there may be emotionally stressful events (like having unwanted psychic experiences, for example). In the OOBE there isn't always a "tunnel", encounters with deceased loved ones are rare, and a "floating" sensation is often reported. Some people who have frequent OOBEs can consciously control where they go during the experience, others cannot.

There is often a "silver cord" mentioned by people who report this experience. It usually attaches at the navel. It's said that when the silver cord is loosened or broken that the spirit leaves the body for good. The silver cord is mentioned in the Bible (Ecclesiastes 12:6).

Is there a Hell?

There are some people who report unpleasant experiences during OOBEs and NDEs, though this is rare. My own experiences were often terrifying. I'd be frozen, unable to move, and dark, shadowy or invisible beings would attack me. Electric shocks coursed through my body. For one two-year period I woke night after night, shaking in terror. I would be awake and aware of my surroundings, but physically still asleep.

Living With Your Psychic Gifts

This condition is called "Sleep Paralysis" by doctors, but I believe there is also a psychic or spiritual component in some cases. My belief is that people who have chronic problems with sleep paralysis are having partial out of body experiences, and they get temporarily stuck in hellish, purgatory-like conditions, what some psychics call the "lower astral". This vibrational condition is populated with fear-based entities, unveiled beings who feed on fear and discontent. That is why these experiences are so frightening. Near death survivors who have these experiences are in a subjective, almost hypnotic state, and if there is a fear-based reaction, their subconscious expectations often give a demonic overlay to them.

If you are raised in a religion that weekly pounds the pulpit with hellfire and damnation sermons, as I was, then it's not surprising that these experiences are horrific. I honestly feel that well-meaning parents are actually behaving in an abusive manner when they drill the fear of God into their children. God is pure love, fear doesn't enter into the picture.

Most people's astral experiences though are positive and pleasant, however. Once I was aware of what was happening, my own experiences became more positive and less frequent. If you find yourself having these experiences, and you are lucid and aware, calm your thoughts. The more you panic, the more you draw negativity in this state. You can try prayer. This did not work for me, but it does work for some people. Try using the white light visualization. Some people have found grounding or affirming that they are a child of the earth to be helpful. When you are awake, quickly splash your feet and hands with cold water, and ground yourself.

Auras and the Etheric Body

Some psychics will tell you they "see" auras, and others "feel" them. The majority will find it hard to describe just exactly what it is they experience, but a few people actually see lights as bright and real to them as the people or objects giving off the aura. For the majority, the experience is more "memory-like". They know the aura and its "colors" are there, but they don't actually see them with their eyes. It's more of a feeling, a mental picture, like memory. When it has happened with me, it is more of a vibration I sense, which I relate to others as colors.

Each of the colors has a distinct interpretation. Darker colors are usually indicators of injury or ill health. Brighter ones can indicate talents or areas of growth, both physical (as in the case of a pregnancy) and mental-spiritual (a bright yellow aura around the head can indicate a highly active intelligence).

Auric damage around the head, neck, lower back and spine is frequently present in hyper-sensitive psychics, especially when they are in a crisis period. Doing the "White Light" meditation can help. If you are a hyper-sensitive and notice holes or gaps in your own aura, do the "White Light" exercise at least three times daily, adding extra light to those "gaps" until you notice they fill in of their own accord.

You may also find that there are sticky cords or lumps of sticky dark matter on your aura at times. Bathing in an Epsom Salt bath (1-2 cups in a tub) with a couple drops of lavender essential oil while doing the White Light exercise can help clear away these "astral cling-ons". If you have this problem a lot, do a "spring cleaning". Get rid of the clutter in your home, in your wardrobe, throw out any clothes you haven't worn in a year, and do a sage and salt cleansing of your home.

The Astral Plane

Whole books have been written on astral travel and out of body experience. There are now online classes that claim to teach you how to get out of your body. The simplest explanation of the astral plane is that it is a dimension of the mind between the "earth-physical" and "heaven-spiritual" planes. Angels, guides and the spirits of the departed, as well as the minds and spirits of living souls, periodically enter this dimension, usually during NDEs, OOBEs, or during the dream state.

There are many classes and lessons purporting to teach the learner how to leave the body at will, to trigger OOBEs and astral experiences, but this is an incredibly rare gift to master. There may yet be a method that is found to be effective, but overall, it is only a few people who have any luck at any particular technique. And it is not a practice that is recommended to the neophyte.

Avoid experimenting with OOBEs and astral travel if you are at all uncomfortable with your intuitive gifts, especially if you feel you may be a hyper-sensitive.

Chapter Six
Shocking Experiences ("Kundalini")

In the spring of 1984 I began to have what I called "The Experiences". In February of that year, I suffered from night after night of bizarre, nightmarish visions, where my body would vibrate, and sensations like an electric shock shot straight up my spine. I would not be able to move. I could only scream in my mind, begging Jesus to make it go away, until I finally awoke, shaking and sweating, terrified. I was often aware I was asleep, but could not stop the "dream". I could only let it play out its course. It was nearly six years later before I truly understood what had happened to me, before I realized that I was not alone in suffering these strange events.

Looking back, it is not surprising that these experiences frightened me. I was raised in a fundamentalist Christian family. Naturally, I interpreted what was happening in the light of those teachings. I frequently cried out to Jesus and prayed incessantly for relief, yet these experiences continued to haunt me almost nightly. It was a time of near panic for me. I had no frame of reference, no convenient jargon to describe what was happening.

My family was unhelpful. The natural conclusion for my mother was that these "Experiences" were the "Work of the Devil". It was not too long after that assessment that "demonic" figures began to appear in the experiences. When I confided in my mother, she suggested that we attend a local "full gospel" church. Perhaps the Holy Spirit could "cure" me of this problem.

We went to the church that weekend. It was a large, non-denominational church, with a very charismatic congregation. My mother had visited only a few times, and we were both unfamiliar with the pastor. I asked the subject of the sermon that night, and my mother said she did not know.

The sermon was "Visions and Dreams, God's Way of Communication".

Needless to say, my mother was not as impressed as I was. She had not been praying for an answer or a sign to that particular dilemma for months, as I had. The sermon was a turning point for me. I truly felt that I had "God's permission" to explore this experience, even though it seemed to be outside the teachings I previously knew. I was determined to find an answer.

Living With Your Psychic Gifts

It was soon afterwards that I met someone who told me that the experience sounded familiar. He mentioned some East Indian teachings, and recommended a book called "The Kundalini Experience" by Dr. Lee Sannella. He also recommended that I put my feet and hands in cold water, and told me about grounding.

I was leery at first. I figured that the exercises couldn't hurt, though, and gave it a try. The experiences still came, but they gradually became less and less frightening. Soon afterward, I met a naturopath who took me seriously enough to actually let me finish my story without reaching for a anti-depressant prescription. He thought that I was trying to "get out of the body". I began to read books on the subject, and discovered some parallels to my own experiences in the works of Robert Monroe ("Journeys Out Of The Body").

When I first learned of Kundalini, and the chakras, I was totally skeptical. I was not interested in the Eastern teachers, especially as I was rapidly becoming ever more disillusioned with anything smacking of organized religion. Still, some of the teachings made sense, in the light of my own experiences. Having no knowledge of the chakras, I had somehow managed to activate them, and I experienced physical sensations in all the major centers.

Living With Your Psychic Gifts

I believe that the energy that the Eastern teachers call Kundalini is the same force that Christians call The Holy Spirit. The Oriental teachers call it Chi. George Lucas described it best in "Star Wars". He simply called it "The Force". All living things use this energy. It is the force of life itself.

Modern physics has begun to prove the ancient idea that all matter is essentially variations on the speed of vibration of a fundamental energy. As human beings, we train ourselves to ignore this vibration, until we consciously arouse it through meditation or prayer. Sometimes we accidentally channel it through the wrong pathways. The effect is something like sticking a fork into an electric socket. There is an electric or physical sensation that some interpret as vibration. There is a rushing sound, like Niagara Falls in the ears. Frequently, the person may see lights or visions, and there may be psychic experiences. Some people display an innate knowledge of yoga postures, even finding themselves involuntarily making yoga gestures at times. In severe cases, the physical nervous system can be literally "burned out". I have seen physical burn marks on the forearms as a result of poor grounding when raising psychic energy. They look like electrical or lightning burns.

Living With Your Psychic Gifts

The chakra system acts like a psychic dam. It filters our responses to every area of our life. When we feel we can't communicate, our throat center may be blocked. If we feel sexually frustrated, we may have one or more blockages in the lower centers. As a psychic, I frequently find that people have blockages in the solar plexus or heart center, and they have been told by doctors that they suffer from "free floating anxiety". Although there is often a physical equivalent, many times a person is simply interpreting vibrating energy as anxiety.

Blockages can be caused by physical, emotional, mental and psychic trauma. Frequently, they are wounds caused by dysfunctional family backgrounds. Sexually abused children often carry their trauma well into adulthood, and some never overcome that wound. A clairvoyant may see the blockage as a hurtful or ugly color surrounding the affected chakra. Most people simply live with an endless string of repetitive disasters, until their discomfort forces them at last to seek help. Usually they come to a psychic or counselor with what appears to be a current problem, only to be told that it's real root lies in an unwillingness to release past trauma.

The affected chakra can only hold so much energy before it must somehow be released. A traumatic event can be stored in the system, like electrical energy is held in a capacitor. Sooner or later there is a discharge of energy. You might call this discharge a "crisis".

A crisis is an opportunity. Few people see their crisis times as times of learning, and fall back into a state of equilibrium, only to experience another crisis again, once the energy builds up.

In order to moderate these energies, it can be helpful to know more about the system, and how it operates.

The Chakras

There is frequent disagreement amongst psychics and religious teachers as to just how many chakras, or centers, or "wheels" of psychic energy exist in the body. Most agree that there are seven major centers, though it seems there are always one or two more new ones with each passing lecture season.

Some mystery schools focus on a chakra at the feet, and others, while acknowledging the center, attribute it to some sort of "evil" activities, and discourage its use. I have found a grounding exercise concerning it that suits me, and feel that there may be a rivalry between two ancient sects that may account for its bad name. I recommend that only serious students of meditation use the foot chakra for anything other than grounding.

The base chakra is associated with the color red in Western new-age teachings. It lies at the base of the spine. It is believed that the Kundalini energy lies dormant at the base of the spine, until intense meditation or psychic activity activates it.

Since most of the people I have met with active Kundalini are ordinary folks, I doubt that intense meditation is a necessary prerequisite. The gurus make much of Kundalini, but you do not have to be a highly spiritual person to activate it. I did it by mistake! At the time this happened to me, I was not particularly spiritually active. Arousing the energy or showing a psychic gift is no guarantee that one is dealing with a "highly evolved spirit", either.

In fact if someone tells you they are "highly evolved", consider that just an indication that they are not (and they are either trying to manipulate you or flatter themselves). I recall a story where one guru said that if a person was a stinker before Kundalini enlightenment, he'd probably be a stinker after, too.

The second center lies at the area of the sexual organs (ovaries/testicles). Its color is orange, and represents the balance between thought and action. Naturally, it relates to sexual functioning as well.

The solar plexus, or sun center, is aptly named, because like the sun, it's energy is bright yellow. Thoughts, ideas, physical power, control and domination come from or through this center. It is frequently misused, therefore it is often blocked. It relates to the digestive and assimilative system in the body.

The heart center vibrates to the color green. Of course, it relates to the higher forms of love, affection, and it rules the physical heart.

The throat center is blue, and reflects our ability to communicate. It rests near the thyroid gland, at the center of the throat.

The next center is often called the "Third Eye". Indigo or deep purple in color, it relates to pure thought, and thus rules psychic ability. It is located between the eyebrows, on the forehead, and is related to the pineal or pituitary gland.

The topmost center, the "thousand petaled lotus" as it is called, is often bright white, violet or pink in color. It is our highest point, our connection with the Divine force. It also relates to the mind, but it connects us with our soul or spiritual self.

I have only scratched the surface here, and there is much that I too need to learn. I myself am not an expert at meditation, and there are books by much more experienced teachers on the subject. There are no shortage of chakra meditation videos and CDs, and many alternatives are available on YouTube.

A basic way to get in touch with the different centers is to try this exercise:

The Rainbow Lotus

Sit in a comfortable position. Relax, as you did for the "white light" exercise. When you are ready, imagine that energy is rising from the earth, traveling up your spine. At the base of the spine, a red flower opens. Feel the warmth from this flower flow up to the sexual center, where a bright orange flower blossoms. Next, the yellow flower at the solar plexus opens, drawing the energy up to the heart, where a lovely green flower blooms. At the throat, a blue flower opens. A beautiful two-petal flower of deep purple opens on the brow, and finally, a huge flower, with too many petals to count, opens above your head. Bask in the glow of this rainbow for a time. Notice any sensations you feel in each of the centers. Take your time. Notice if one particular flower seems blocked or difficult to open. If so, send healing pink or golden light into the center of the flower until it gently eases open. Finally, imagine yourself surrounded with a lovely white light glow. See the energy slowly flow down your body, back into the earth. As it does, each flower closes in turn, holding a tiny seed of bright light. "Ground" yourself. Slowly move your body, stretch, and allow the image to fade from your mind. If you feel you need extra grounding, dip your feet and hands in cold water.

Remember, meditation can bring in more energy than you may want. It is a good idea to meditate with a group of experienced mediators at first. That way, you can get feedback on your progress, and learn more about meditation from people with firsthand experience. You will also find the resulting effects to be more powerful and noticeable when you meditate in groups of people. A local Buddhist centre or temple may offer free courses, and paid classes are often available as night-school courses in community colleges. If you feel the signs of mis-aligned psychic energy, discontinue any meditation (except for the grounding practice) and follow a regular diet for a time.

Always remember to ground your energy.

I recommend that serious students dig deeper on the subject of meditation. I have only scratched the surface here. Finding a qualified instructor can make a huge difference in your progress. If you would like a recommendation though, check out James Roswell Quinn's "Centering" meditation exercises on his web site at www.lovebasedleader.com.

"Astral Catalepsy"

In Sylvia Browne's book *"Visits from the AfterLife"*, she described something she calls "Astral Catalepsy", which sounds similar to Kundalini or sleep paralysis disorders (see page 24 in her book).

Her theory was that the soul is partly getting out of the body, and that the experiences are caused by a combination of physical and psychic effects sounds a lot like sleep paralysis to me. I wasn't her biggest fan, but in this case, I do believe she was right. On one occasion I was told by a chiropractor that the problem was that

I was trying to get out of the body but I was getting stuck halfway through the process.

I believe that fear and blockages in our chakra systems are what causes "astral catalepsy", though this may be triggered by food and some pharmaceutical drugs as well.

UFOs & Sleep Paralysis

The UFO phenomenon is controversial, and it seems there are only two entrenched sides to the debate. Either you believe firmly that space aliens are kidnapping people through the walls of their bedrooms, or you think that the whole thing is some kind of fringe psychological phenomena (to put it in the kindest, most politically correct terms).

There are an extremely small number of cases that seem to defy the psychological explanation. When there is physical evidence left behind, for example: strange clothing that appears after an experience, lost time, unexplained radiation or unidentifiable metals imbedded in the bodies of the participants. But such cases are rare. Looking at the bulk of the stories though, it seems kind of obvious that what is going on in the vast majority of these cases is another form of the sleep paralysis phenomena.

Sleep paralysis is a relatively rare and poorly understood phenomenon, but it happens when the mind awakes while the body is still asleep. When we sleep, the body is paralyzed by processes that are in place to keep up from acting out our dreams. It's sort of the opposite of sleep walking. In both cases, the "switch" is flipped at the wrong time.

I have experienced "sleep paralysis" on numerous occasions. I have never encountered space creatures, but I have had encounters with unknown entities in this state. I believe that sleep paralysis may be either a factor in, or a symptom of psychic awakening in many cases.

Sleep paralysis is a form of sleeping disorder that affects a small number of people, a great many of whom do seem to be sensitive psychically. It starts with the person waking up paralyzed, unable to move, often with a buzzing noise or vibration in their heads, similar to the Kundalini energies.

Some people experience this as often as every night, but more often it comes on during stressful periods. In some cases there are profoundly realistic visionary experiences, but this is not always the case. Some sleep paralysis victims identify their experiences as dreams.

Others cannot differentiate them from reality. There were times I found it difficult to tell the difference. it was only when certain unreal elements would come in that I could determine that I had been asleep. The colors, sounds, smells and memories often seem much more striking than waking consciousness, more real than reality.

The people, beings, and experiences that abductees claim to meet may in fact have at least a partial foundation in another realm of reality. I have also had astral experiences, and believe that some of these experiences are objectively real. Information gained through some astral experiences can often be verified independently by others.

The beings on these planes of reality can be neutral, good or evil. I believe they may in fact reside on the astral level or some vibration between the astral and our waking reality. It is entirely possible that beings on another dimensional plane have figured out a way to cross dimensional barriers, or may be doing it accidentally just as we so often do.

In the astral plane, many beings do have the ability to "shape shift", to mask their true appearance in this state. All you have to do is think about something and you can make it real.

Living With Your Psychic Gifts

The more aware you are, the more control you can have over your surroundings.

Because most human beings are only minimally aware, we have very little control over astral experiences. Worse, human beings have this tendency to project a layer of their own expectations onto astral experiences. The challenge is to distinguish what your mind makes up, and what really comes to you from the outside. The whole experience is a combination of "reality" and "expectations", and it is often colored by cultural and religious expectations. I encountered "demons" in my early experiences, which gradually disappeared or transformed into much more positive forms as I grew in comfort and understanding.

When the abduction phenomena is combined with sensations of flight, traveling through walls, strange vibrations, awakening paralyzed, with strange lights, the likelihood is high that the participant is also experiencing sleep paralysis. If this is happening to you, seek out a sleep clinic and be tested for sleep apnea, because it can be related to sleep paralysis. Symptoms of apnea include heavy snoring and waking up gulping for air. Apnea can be life threatening in extreme cases.

Both apnea and sleep paralysis are hard to treat, but can be managed with a CPAP machine, lifestyle, dietary and pharmaceutical changes. Sleep paralysis can be made worse by sleep deprivation, stress, drug interactions and caffeine. I found that when I mixed Tylenol 1 with an antihistamine I got the most ugly forms of this phenomenon.

Dr. Jorge Conesa finds "statistically significant effects of changes in the geomagnetic flux and the reported incidence of sleep paralysis"[1], and I recall I had more of these incidents in Vancouver than in Toronto, so moving from highly-charged areas might be a solution if nothing else works. This correlation could explain why there are large numbers of reports in psychically-charged areas like Arizona, Colorado, British Columbia, etc. It makes some sense that electro-magnetic energy could interfere with sleep. I also found that dipping my feet and hands in cold water immediately after the experience prevented them from recurring as frequently.

---

[1] http://www.geocities.ws/jorgeconesa/Paralysis/sleepnew.html

Chapter Seven
Addressing Concerns of
Family, Friends, Church & Others

When you first begin to explore your psychic potential, you may find yourself at odds with certain people who do not share your experiences or understanding about psychic phenomena. There is a lot of fear, based on false negative stereotypes advanced by Hollywood, horror novels, skeptics and religions. It may be hard to accept, but the path to self-understanding can be a lonely one, particularly when your closest friends and family have different opinions.

It would be wonderful if I could report that most people I know say they experienced enthusiastic responses from family and friends when relating their experiences. It is difficult enough to be coming to grips with a life altering experience, but when a strong religious or atheist background meets up with a spontaneous psychic awakening, emotional chaos is almost always the result. You may not have to abandon your religious beliefs to integrate your psychic experience, but you may need to rethink key issues before you resolve them.

Please Practice
SAFE SECTS

Religion, science, advertising, the Internet and the media have proven conclusively that accepting beliefs on faith can be hazardous to your sanity and well being

http://www.cafepress.com/bjasmine/237906

I was raised in a fundamentalist Pentecostal Christian family. While many of the things I now believe are at least somewhat endorsed by that church, many are not. I studied Biblical history and the Bible for years in order to resolve my personal doubts and fears, and if you are Christian, I highly recommend that you do so as well, if you are feeling doubts. A sincere study of the scriptures and history of your faith may prove to be essential. I personally found that many things taught in church have no basis in the scriptures, once you factor in translations, grammatical and historic context. Many psychics that I know come from Christian families. They attend church, and regard their ability as the gift of "discernment". Where they may differ from the "orthodox" point of view, is the strongly held conviction that all religions have a Divine spark. Each contains "Truth". Religion is simply another language to describe the Indescribable.

Living With Your Psychic Gifts

I get many letters from people who have been frightened by their "psychic" experiences because they have been taught that these are "gifts of the devil". There is a simple way to deal with that fear. Take the word "psychic" and replace it with "The Holy Spirit". These are merely two different ways of describing the same experience, from different points of view. If you look at Paul's descriptions of the "Gifts of the Spirit", they are the same as the psychic gifts.

To one there is given through the Spirit the message of wisdom, to another the message of knowledge by means of the same Spirit, to another faith by the same Spirit, to another gifts of healing by that one Spirit, to another miraculous powers, to another prophecy, to another distinguishing between spirits

(1 Corinthians 12)

When I have a "psychic impression" and feel called to warn or assist a Christian friend, I say that the Holy Spirit is prompting me to mention something, and I find it is usually then received without fear. I also tell Christian and former Christian psychics to say that the "Holy Spirit moved me to tell you that ..." if they are not comfortable with saying "psychic", or fear reactions from friends and family. The only real difference is that I believe that psychic gifts are a natural part of human talents, and most Christians believe that these talents come from God. I can reconcile that by saying that ultimately, the Divine has given us all our talents, so yes, they are gifts from God.

Doctors, Medicine and Metaphysics

A lot of the people who write to me express the fear that if they tell a doctor about their psychic experiences, they will be labeled as "crazy".

This is not an irrational fear, especially if the doctor in question has a lot of authority in your community. I have heard of people losing jobs, children, and even their freedom as a result of an unfair diagnosis of mental illness, but to be fair, this is quite rare. There is usually some other additional cause for the person's trouble.

In one case, a woman following the Wiccan religion had her children taken away, but this was primarily a result of the persistent activity of her ex-husband, who I believe would have found some other excuse if this one was not handy. There is no argument that an injustice was done to her, but few of the other Wicca in her community need to fear seizure of their children. There were other factors at work that made her a target.

If you live in a large city, have good family support and are not marginalized in some social or political way, you have little to fear from being honest with others about your psychic experiences or beliefs. If you are poor, are a visible minority, practice alternative faith or lifestyle choices, have a dysfunctional family, or have a history of erratic or criminal behavior, you could find it is a lot more risky to speak out. That is the reality of our profoundly dysfunctional, prejudiced society.

If you want to speak to your current doctor and are not sure what their reaction might be, you might be able to find non-threatening ways to bring the topic up. I was seeing a specialist who had some Egyptian paintings displayed. I started speaking to her about the goddesses and their meanings, and that conversation allowed me to mention some of my experiences. She proved to be very open and accepting. In other cases, my intuition told me to avoid mentioning the psychic aspects of my life. Instead, I focused on the purely physical symptoms, emotions, or used psychological terms instead of psychic ones to describe a particular symptom.

If you are not comfortable with speaking to your current doctor honestly, then you may have the wrong doctor, and it is a good idea to shop around discretely for a new one. Make a few appointments, interview them, and ask them flat out what they would think if a patient admitted to having a psychic experience. If they are skeptical, can they put that aside in order to treat you objectively? If they are uncomfortable, then thank them for their time and make another appointment. Ask friends and family members for referrals to their doctors.

If you are absolutely unable to change doctors, then you may have to make the choice not to bring the subject up - and the truth is, it might not be necessary. You can share fears, anxieties and other symptoms without speaking about your psychic experiences.

However ... if you are depressed, suicidal, or if you are hearing voices that berate you, put you down, or tell you to do things that you know are wrong, do NOT hold back this information from your doctor!

There is no legitimate spiritual guide that would behave in this manner. There are only two possibilities in such a case. Either you have attracted a nasty spirit, or you do in fact have a mental illness, or both. If you cannot get rid of the voice or voices by drawing on the psychic protections in this book, then the chances are excellent you could greatly benefit from medical treatment. Don't risk your well being, and the happiness of your family. Get help at once. Some medications (such as Prozac) can be effective at shutting down unwanted psychic experiences. They have their risks and benefits, and all have side effects. Discuss the options with your doctor.

Dealing with Skeptics

One of the common challenges for the beginning psychic or intuitive is dealing with friends, family, and even strangers who are skeptical of your experiences and beliefs. Many start off feeling insecure and uncertain. I get many questions asking me "Am I really psychic?" when it is clear from their experiences that they have had many psychic events. I think the reason for this is that they have encountered a lot of skepticism.

I'm probably one of the most skeptical believers that I know of. In fact some have accused me of not being supportive because I have challenged their assumptions on my discussion group. When I ask a participant to consider another possibility that may not be psychic to explain their experiences, I'm not necessarily saying that they don't have psychic ability. What I am saying is that not every insight, a dream, or vision necessarily needs to be interpreted as psychic. It is too easy to get wrapped up in wishful or magical thinking and this leads to the high level of anxiety that plagues many psychics, especially in the beginning. It is concern for their well being that leads me to challenge their assumptions.

While it is a good thing to be skeptical, it is a different matter altogether to identify yourself as being "a skeptic". This to me indicates that your identity and therefore ego is engaged, you start with the assumption that the topic is bogus, and it is your intention is to disprove it. That's not how it is supposed to be, but in practice this is how most self-identified "skeptics" behave. A scientist may take a theory, and to devise experiments to test that theory, but a true scientist is obliged to keep an open mind and follow where the evidence leads, not to compose an argument to defend a established opinion. Unfortunately, there are few scientists worthy of the name who identify themselves as skeptics.

Some skeptics point to the fact that psychics aren't 100% accurate all times to justify their skepticism. One thing they say is that extraordinary claims demand extraordinary proof. But they fail to notice that almost no one is really claiming 100% accuracy (outside of the obvious frauds, that is). What we're claiming is psychic ability, and what they say we're claiming is omniscience. Anyone who has psychic ability is subject to the same human frailties and biases as every other human being. This has to be factored into the equation. I have found in my work as an intuitive that the intuitive impressions are always accurate. It is my interpretation that may be off base.

There is a delightful movie called "The Butcher's Wife", starring Demi Moore, that illustrates this problem beautifully (spoiler alert). The lead character is a sensitive and beautiful psychic who has a vision of her destined mate rowing up on her island home in a rowboat. She throws herself into the first rowboat she sees, covers the hapless butcher in enthusiastic kisses, marries him, and flits off to New York with him ... and of course he was the wrong guy! I won't spoil any more of the story for you, but it's definitely worth the rental. Whoever wrote the screenplay for "The Butcher's Wife" knows a lot about us intuitives.

Only someone who has worked with intuition over an extended periods of time can truly appreciate these challenges. We all like to think that we are intelligent, rational and capable of seeing clearly, and while that's usually true, in highly emotional circumstances, we can often be unconsciously led astray by our desires, biases and subconscious motivations. Psychics are not immune from this process.

Those who are new to exploring their psychic ability often make the mistake of assuming that the process is perfect. They may experience some success with precognition, and assume that all of their dreams are literal rather than symbolic representations of life events. If the psychics are confused, that it's no wonder that many skeptics are confused as well.

I often find in my discussion group online that beginners are offended when I suggest that they have a look at their dreams and visions as symbolic in addition to or instead of literal representations of events. They seem to think that I'm saying that they're not psychic. That isn't what I'm saying at all. I'm saying that there is a higher, deeper, more profound meaning found in interpreting these experiences symbolically than there is in viewing them automatically as precognitive. In fact, for most of us, dreams are rarely precognitive. Many psychics, both beginners and advanced, allow a longer and longer time frame for events to match up with their dreams are visions. This is a common mistake that many skeptics

Living With Your Psychic Gifts

(legitimately in my opinion) point to as a rational failing in many psychics. If a dream or a vision is not reflected in current events within a 3 to 4 day period, than the dream or vision should be interpreted symbolically and applied to the dreamer or visionary's life. The exception to this could be when there is a persistent repeated pattern of dreaming that takes place over a long period of time, and eventually culminates in the circumstances reflected in the dream or vision. This is extremely rare, and these dreams or visions are often likewise symbolic rather than literal, but it can happen.

The challenge for both teacher and student in exploring intuitive and psychic ability is that human ego is integrally enmeshed in the psychic process. Bluntly, many students who assume that all of their dreams are precognitive are wrapped up in an ego blanket. They want to believe that they have a great power, that this makes them special, unique or wise. The reality is that just about all human beings have some level of psychic ability. Having psychic ability does not make us wise or spiritually superior to others. In my opinion, this is the greatest danger for those who are new to exploring this path.

The challenge in speaking to skeptics is that it is rare to find a skeptic who understands any of this. Few of them have spent much time exploring their own consciousness in a conscious, rational, analytical way. Most have taken a rational rather than a psychological approach to this object. They start with their own bias, objections, and in some cases hostility to the topic. This can make communication difficult. It is a treat and a pleasure to meet that rare skeptic who truly wants to understand why I would believe what I believe.

I do not recommend that psychics take on skeptics in public forums and discussion groups or through the media. I have been invited to skeptical gatherings and have refused them all. Often they are set up like traps. I remember one group that wanted to know why I had declined. I told them I would be a fool to present myself for what would likely be little more than a "gotcha" experiment. I explained that I did not claim omniscience, that a good psychic can be fooled by an organized effort, and that I wasn't interested in playing this game with them. There was no further response.

I'd be more than happy to participate in a legitimate study. I have heard of one or two serious attempts, but these are rare exceptions. Most of the studies or experiments done focus on disproving, debunking or ridiculing the phenomenon, or in embarrassing the psychics involved, rather than seeking to understand the phenomena better.

When people approach me as skeptics, I tell them that I respect their beliefs, but their opinions are just that, opinions. They don't have my experiences, they don't know what I know, and my experience is that the exercise of debating the subject is a waste of time.

If skeptics approach me with the attitude that they wish to understand better why I believe what I believe, then I'm happy to talk to them and explain it, but in reality this almost never happens. I usually get insulting, hostile, negative attacks, and these people don't understand why I don't want to talk to them?

I suggest you don't talk to them, either. Carry on in your own path for now. If you are kidding yourself, your journal-keeping will reveal that to you in time.

Living With Your Psychic Gifts

Chapter Eight
Dealing with Psychic Children

I was a psychic child. Looking back, I can remember several events, deja vu, stories that I wrote for school classes that later seemed to predict events in my own life. I would mention an old TV episode, and it would be rerun later that week (that kind of thing still happens quite a lot). Yet I did not make the connection between my history as a "sensitive child" and my psychic experiences until many years later.

Some Signs of the Psychic Child:

- unexplained hyperactivity or withdrawal
- vivid and persistent imaginary playmates
- precognitive dreams
- an apparent connection between the child's behavior and a parent's emotions.
- seeing auras or colors around people
- recalling past lives
- emotional sensitivity
- the loner, the outsider, a target of peer abuse
- challenges in social interactions
- creativity beyond the norm in art and/or music

Psychic children are extremely sensitive. They frequently experience the emotions of others and mistake them for their own. The emotions that playmates may have when teasing or playing can impact strongly on a young child who cannot distinguish between her feelings and those of others. As a result, they are frequently targets for peer abuse and bullying.

Many times I felt that other children at school hated me, when it was their own self-loathing or dysfunctional family energy I was picking up on. "Sensitive" children need to have their intuitions and feelings validated, especially if there is bullying, teasing or hurtful behavior directed at them, and this is often the case. These kids are different, they attract attention.

When this happens, I recommend you take the child aside and say: "Gee, honey, I know that you're feeling hurt right now. I think I'd feel that way too, if that happened to me. When you feel better, we can talk about it again." Let them have a good cry, hug them, but don't insist they get over it immediately. Once the child is calmer, and they know you understand, you can better discuss ways to cope with any inappropriate behavior.

Too often sensitive children are told "Don't feel that way". A sensitive child interprets this as a judgment on those feelings, not as concern for them. Rather than hearing that you wish them to be happy, they hear that your emotional comfort is more important than theirs ("Feel good so I won't have to feel bad"). That is a terrific burden for a young child to carry. Sensitive children learn to bury their feelings, rather than express them, but children can no more turn off feelings than adults can. Those emotions come out later as "acting out" or even later in life as emotional scars, which can be as intense and dramatic as those in physically abused children.

If you do not know what to say to your child to make things better, remember one simple tip: Ask, don't tell. Don't try to analyze their behavior or that of their peers. if they seem to be too sensitive, instead of saying so, ask "What makes you feel that way?" Ask leading questions, guide them to figuring out the solution on their own. Or just hug them and let them cry through it. Be honest, tell them the fact that they are hurting hurts you, and you don't know what to say.

Unfortunately, a history of childhood peer abuse is common amongst psychics. Highly sensitive children can find the politics of the school yard difficult to master. They tend to be more creative, imaginative and intelligent than average, and these qualities can make them prime targets for bullies (and abusive teachers or administrators).

Living With Your Psychic Gifts

If your child is being bullied at school, whether they are psychic or not, you cannot sit back and allow the abuse to go on. Peer abuse can leave a lifetime of scars. There are some terrific books and online resources that can help you cope.

I am an adult survivor of bullying, and while my position may sound extreme to some parents, I believe if you do not have support from school authorities in ending peer abuse, then the only alternative may be to pull your child out of school. Affordable homeschooling resources are easily available online, and homeschooled children often do as well or better than children in public schools. I can understand concerns about socialization. I share some of those concerns, as a big part of the problem is the sensitive's need for better coping skills, but there are healthier and affordable alternatives available. It is more important to stop the abuse. Personal growth classes, church groups, sport and arts clubs all provide excellent opportunities to learn good social skills.

If you suspect that you have a psychic child on your hands, keep an open mind, but remember, a psychic gift is no guarantee of spiritual genius. Too much interest can be more damaging than indifference. The high expectations of a parent can be impossible for a child to live up to, and there is the danger of pride or arrogance.

Don't make a psychic child perform psychic tricks for others. If they are not interested, they may feel that you are putting them on display – and you are. It will only make them feel more different than they already do. If your child does express an interest, as well as the talent, you can encourage them share with you, or to keep a journal of their own. For a young child, you may do this yourself, writing down the strange things the child says, the stories about imaginary friends, and the feelings that came true. Write down as much information as you can, including the time and date if possible.

Once your child realizes that you are open minded about the subject, that you don't think they are "weird", they may have a lot of questions. Honesty is always the best policy. I would approach the subject with the same tact I would when approaching the subject of sex. Wait for the child to ask you questions. "Active Listening" techniques are an excellent tool for parents to cut through resistance and communicate better with your sensitive child.

Always answer honestly. If you don't know an answer, say so, and follow up by finding information. The Internet has many good articles and web sites available on a wide variety of psychic subjects. Call your favorite psychic and ask questions. Simple E.S.P. "games" can be tried, like "Remote Viewing" experiments. Ask on my discussion group, or send me an email on the contact form at www.psychicprotection.net.

Monster Spray

One of the participants of my discussion group came up a with a terrific idea for helping children cope with seeing spirits. She bought her kids a bottle of "Monster Spray". It was nothing but a spray bottle with some food color and glitter in it, but it helped them overcome a challenging and common fear. They sprayed it around the room and felt better.

It's possible that the "monster under the bed" or in the closet may well have a real spiritual foundation. Children see spirits more easily than adults do, and they may tune into the fears of these entities. What seems mild and unobtrusive to an adult can be scary to a young child. I would make my own magic spray adding some lemon juice, a few bay leaves, and some essential oils (lemon grass, lavender or sage oil, no more than 5-10 drops per bottle). The energy of the herbs and oils will lighten the energy, and just knowing you take their fears seriously should be helpful to the child.

Chapter Nine
Finding a Good Psychic
First - Know Thyself

Such was the command above the command above the Oracle at Delphi. Priests and kings often consulted this famous medium, but seldom did they come seeking wisdom of their inner selves. Like most modern people who seek out psychic advice, they came to discover "The Future". They wanted to know what battles to wage, what goals to pursue in love and war. Modern psychics will tell you from experience that nothing has changed.

People still come to find out when they will marry, what job is best, if they will ever be rich. I am often asked how to find a "good" psychic. There are a few "good psychics" and lots of not so good ones. It can be confusing to pick one, especially at a psychic fair where literally dozens of psychics offer a bewildering variety of services.

In order to find a good psychic you must first know your own needs. Legitimate, professional psychics focus on the personality and core issues of the client, rather than looking exclusively at "the future". This can be a bit distracting to the client who has come for a bit of "fortune telling". Serious psychics consider "fortune telling" to be mere entertainment, and some refuse to consider the future at all. Often, they advertise themselves as "intuitive consultants", "psychic counselors" or "advisors". You must decide what is more important, entertainment, or knowing yourself and your life more clearly. Obviously, I favor the latter. But one of the things that attracted me to this field is that I love to peek into the future.

Forecasts are still part of a good psychic reading. They certainly are the most entertaining part. But if a reading is to have lasting value beyond entertainment, it must make a difference in the client's life. When I worked as an intuitive consultant, forecasts came in the middle of a reading, after I had analyzed my thoughts and feelings about my client. I looked at the person as they were in the "now". I looked at their strengths and weaknesses, the energy in their life "today", and then I projected that energy forward. I usually looked ahead for a few months at most.

I believe that you do create your own future to a great degree, and that the choices you make today can profoundly affect the way your future takes shape. If the reading is effective, the predictions may or may not come true. If the reading alters your future, hopefully it will be because you have seen your choices clearly in that session. You may decide to change your course of action. Frequently, I could see that possibility, and let my client know about their choices, and how each choice will impact their life. The point of the reading is to give the client a clear reflection of his or her life right now. It is this moment that affects the future you will live. It was my hope that my clients walked away from a reading feeling empowered, realizing that they could create their future.

Each psychic chose his or her method of reading because it fit with his or her own personality, philosophy or needs. Often, the style of reading will itself indicate something of what motivates the psychic. Each system has its own strengths and weaknesses, as each psychic will. Tarot readers often find it difficult to time events, for example. Astrology can be very precise, but it requires an analytical mind with a good memory for details. Some astrologers choose this tool because they do not wish to be so intimate with their clients. The chart stands in place of the person, giving them a comfort zone they might not have if they had to physically examine hands like a palmist does.

You should decide what you want, and what you are willing to pay, before you go for a reading. It is a good idea to bring a list of questions to the reading. Let the reading flow naturally, and listen to what the psychic says about you, before you ask any questions. That way, you can know if you are "connecting" with that person. Look at James Van Praugh the next time he appears on a television show. I have noticed that he takes special pains to interrupt people if they reveal too much, because it invalidates the process.

A good psychic usually starts with events that they feel are still unfolding now. They look at finances, love life and work. They make predictions after they have established a pattern. At that point, they may ask: "Now, do you have any questions you would like to ask?" At this point a good psychic will be gifted with a bemused expression that tells her that she has already answered most of what the client came to know. It is then time to recap or clarify minor details. Sometimes a significant question or aspect of it will come to mind. It does help to think of a few questions ahead of time, because it clears your mind, making it that much easier to read.

I have had the rare client that I felt I could not connect with in a way that satisfied me. In every case, I discovered that the client was skeptical, or only minimally interested, and usually this resulted from loved ones urging them to come.

Living With Your Psychic Gifts

If my client is a lukewarm person, uninterested in the results of the reading, that will come back reflected in the reading. A vague reading may not reflect the talents of a reader if it accurately reflects your own state of mind! If you feel, however, that you aren't connecting, or are uncomfortable, then say so, and walk away. It makes no sense to waste your time and your psychic's by playing games like "Can you read my mind?" It is obvious when there is a connection. Speak up! If you don't, then it is only fair to pay the reader for her time. She may or may not be a fraud, but if you come on false pretenses, who are you to judge?

Keep in mind too that a psychic will tell you what he or she finds interesting about you, not always what you are interested in. Psychics are human too, and can be deflected from an important issue by their own biases. If you feel this is happening, then tell your psychic that there is another matter that interests you more. If you are clear about what you want to know, then the psychic will be clearer relating it to you. If there seems to be a problem, it may be that your personal ideas about yourself don't harmonize well with the opinion of the psychic. The psychic may get all the facts right, but misinterpret your feelings about them.

Living With Your Psychic Gifts

It may also be possible that the psychic is on to something, and you are resisting it. "Resistance" and "Denial" are jargon words that psychics and psychologists use when they feel that they are getting at the truth, but the client will not, or cannot admit it consciously. If you experience an emotional reaction to a statement you consciously believe to be untrue, there may well be some truth in what was said. These lessons are often the most difficult to learn.

I once encountered a young woman involved in an abusive relationship. She admitted at first that there was something horribly wrong, and I foresaw that the only real solution was for her to leave, and the sooner the better. It seemed to be what her mate wanted all along, but she stubbornly clung to the relationship. I told her that the situation would become dangerous if she would not leave. "I'm going to MAKE it work," she insisted.

Finally exhausted by her resistance to my suggestions, I suggested she see another psychic. She simply told me to shuffle the cards so she could ask again! I told her another reading by me with different cards would not change the facts, and finally she left when I refused to take her money.

The next day, after the fair, about two dozen psychics got together for dinner. Many of them were relating tales of the different readings they'd done that weekend. I listened as one psychic, who I did not know at the time, related a tale about a client that he had seen that day. She said, "I'm going to MAKE it work!" he said with exasperation. I was floored. Comparing notes and descriptions, we came to the conclusion that this was the same woman. Then two other psychics piped up ... they had seen her as well, and every one had given her the same advice. I fear the message never got through.

We were very different as people and different kinds of psychics, yet we all gave her the same information. If you find yourself resisting something in a reading, ask yourself why. Resistance always has meaning.

Fraudulent psychics

There are usually clear indications from the beginning, if you know what to look for. Some of these signs are so clear, that a fraudulent reader might as well put up a sign saying "RIPOFFS HERE". Study the information or literature that the reader has available. Be on the lookout for any psychic who seems to be trying deliberately to cultivate a "gypsy fortune teller" image or makes extraordinary claims.

I have worked next to true gypsy readers and have heard tales both good and bad, just like everyone else. However, those who try too hard to cultivate such an image are more often interested in show business than in serious substance. This often goes together with outrageous claims: "Madame So-n-So... Knows All...Sees All" If Madame So-n-So knows ALL...what's she doing selling readings at the Psychic Fair for $20? Worst of all - I have encountered so-called "gypsy psychics" who are not even gypsies - so they end up giving true gypsy psychics a bad name, while exploiting a mysterious image in the popular imagination.

The Curse Scam

Unfortunately, fraud artists have other ways to supplement their incomes. If any psychic speaks to you of "curses", and offers to remove them for a fee, I suggest you grab your pocketbook and head for an exit. I would tell such a person that I don't believe in curses, but I do know a scam when I hear one. If I had not yet paid, I would not offer to. If you are at a psychic fair, and something like this happens to you, report the incident to the fair management. In big psychic fairs you will be refunded any money paid, and the reader will be fined or expelled. The promoter has an interest in running a "clean" fair, and will want to know if anyone is "scamming" this way. It is fraud, and it's against the law. "Curses" are nothing but a prelude to an escalating series of demands by the reader who will charge to remove them. Of course the curse is purely imaginary, but a client's life can become a living hell if you choose to believe in one.

One psychic told me a story of a local client who went to a reader who convinced her that her problems with romance were caused by a "curse on her love life". A national TV talk show exposed such scams, complete with magic tricks to show the client how "evil the curse was". There would be a hairball inside an unbroken egg to prove a client was cursed. As silly as this sleight-of-hand image seems, two of the clients taken for a $10,000 ride were well-educated urban professionals. In a vulnerable, highly emotional state, it can be easy to convince even highly educated professionals that they have been "cursed".

When the client ran out of money, the psychic suggested that she be allowed to use her Visa card to pay for her "services". This woman was not "cursed" at all. When helped to see that her issue was a co-dependency problem, I am sure she began the road to recovery. Deep issues like co-dependency or adult child difficulties cannot be cured by a magic wave or gesture. A serious person must seek out competent help, and be willing to work things through.

There are other scams, "blessed" candles that sell for outrageous amounts of money (anything over $30 unless the candle is huge, or is an art-piece), "exorcisms" and other questionable practices. Many practices that I might consider fraudulent at worst, or useless at best, are held in high esteem by some, but you can bless your own candles, and you should learn how to clear the energy in your home. If you feel that you need these services, try to find them on a donation basis, or at a reasonable fee. I would want to pay a psychic for her time, and I would judge how much time it takes to "clear" a space, and pay her at the same rate as her readings. If you wish to pay more out of the goodness of your heart or gratitude that is one thing. But if you feel you have to pay her because you are afraid she will "curse" you, that is something different altogether.

There are two schools of thought where it comes to psychic services. One might say that it is wrong to charge at all. People who hold this view think that the psychic gift is a "holy" one, and should not be a business. I argue that a painter or a doctor has a divine gift too, and just as rightly deserves a reward for their time and knowledge – just not an outrageous one.

What can you expect to pay?

Fair fees range from $30 to $300. The more popular a psychic is, the more expensive his or her rates are going to be. Don't assume that because a psychic is high priced that he or she is going to be good, though. I know of one a-list psychic who was charging $300 an hour for her readings. Late in her career she had to deal with a lot of public criticism and controversy, and I always felt uncomfortable with her. I felt most people wanted to see her and were willing to pay the price, simply for the ability to say they had a reading with her.

There are many reasons for different fees, popularity is only one of them. A visiting psychic may have to charge more. After all, there are hotel and travel expenses to consider. It is not taboo to consider a tip, if you are extremely pleased by the reading.

The local psychic or holistic fair is a good place to comparison shop. You can discover who the local readers are, or see a visiting psychic who you can't see locally. Use your own psychic ability when you shop for a psychic. When you walk around, notice who catches your eye. If you feel bad about someone, trust your first impression. They may be a good reader, but they may not be right for you. The fair is also a good place to have a reading if you have never been to a psychic, and it is well worth the cost of a "mini" reading to find a good psychic. When you book an appointment, arrive a minute or two early, or you may get bumped for the person who waits near the booth.

Most psychics at a reputable fair will have recorders on hand. Some charge for this service, others include it in the cost of a reading. You will be amazed at just how much you forget. If the psychic does not offer recordings, ask if you can use the recording device on your cell phone to record the reading. Most smartphones have that capability built in.

You will know right away if you are "connecting. The psychic will bring up situations that you can identify immediately. A good reading will confirm what you already know in your heart. It will clarify your options, but do not expect your psychic to make choices for you. Your advisor is human too, with human hopes, dreams, and biases. Bear this in mind with any counselor.

Chapter Ten
"The Occult"

I feel compelled to address the issue of "The Occult" here, and to separate the issues of "witchcraft" and "devil worship". First of all, the word "occult" has become a catchall phrase in our culture, a word that people apply to a wide range of unrelated and primarily negative spiritual practices.

In reality occult simply means "hidden", and implies secret beliefs or religions. Every religion has an "occult" wing, or part of the knowledge that is generally kept hidden from the average person. Jewish Occultists are often called Qabbalists or Kabbalists. Christian Occultists are frequently called Witches, Masons, or Magicians.

Most occultists do not worship the Devil. Most are interested in studying Astrology, Numerology, or Tarot, and the ancient scriptures and beliefs that are not part of Sunday School lessons. Frequently, they study the Bible, the Apocrypha and may in fact consider themselves Christians or at least scholars of Biblical history. It is extremely rare that they go out in search of "converts" since most occultists believe that everyone should come to their own enlightenment without any formal religion. Occultists do not generally call themselves "witches". Those who do call themselves witches do so for a variety of reasons, but a good many who do so have a twisted and unrealistic idea of what that means.

There is a legitimate religion called Wicca, whose practitioners call themselves witches. These people worship a goddess as well as a god, and celebrate the earth and changes of the seasons. They may consider themselves neo-pagans, and attempt to live as natural a life as possible. Witches do not worship a Devil, but history records that the image of their Horned God was taken over by Christian propagandists during the witch burnings.

Some groups that identify themselves as "Satanic" use terms like "witch" or "occult", to define themselves, but much of "Satanism" is really a creation of a combination of religious misinformation promulgated by false media and religious stereotypes. It is a myth that has become a sad, twisted reality. There are a few sick individuals who have invented horrible rituals, almost all of them based upon movie or television plots. People that get involved in such practices usually act out of mental illness, ignorance, immaturity, or a frustration with organized religion. They have nothing to do with true "occult", "Wiccan" or "new-age" practices. There is an actual Church of Satan, and some satanic groups are actually more political satire than true religious organizations.

If you are interested in studying the issue, there are a few things to keep in mind. First, remember that most of the books you may read on the subject are for "public consumption". They will usually be simplistic, requiring a discerning mind to read between the lines. Take nothing at face value, until you verify it for yourself. Secondly, be aware of the many "cult" groups. I would have grave doubts about any group that requires its members to give up their worldly goods, for example. Those goods end up furnishing the house of the leader. Christian equivalents exist. Recall Jim and Tammy?

Hidden knowledge promised seldom meets expectations. Ask around. Follow your gut feelings. Bring along a skeptical friend to meetings, do not attend alone.

Remember, if it looks too good to be true, it likely is. Your best defense is an open, but discerning mind. Just because a religious teaching, idea or mental exercise works for one person does not mean it works for everybody. That advice extends even to this book. Take what you feel is valid, and discard the rest.

Living With Your Psychic Gifts

Chapter Eleven
Ghosts, Spirits, Channeling

Here we tread cautiously into what is frightening material for some. The topics of ghosts, spirits, and channeling all brush up on the subject of death, and what we believe about death makes a significant impact on our feelings about the spiritual realm.

I believe that the human spirit survives death. When it comes naturally, in old age, in comforting surroundings, human spirits easily move on into what I call "The Realm of Light", what many call "Heaven". When death comes suddenly or violently, or after long illness, however, spirits are often trapped closer to the physical world than the realm of Light. When this happens, there is often "ghostly" activity, from "cold spots" in certain areas, unexplained mists, electrical disturbances, to more overt manifestations like voices and movement of special items in the home.

Many "ghosts" are simply the impressions of strong feelings left behind when someone dies. A few are actually what psychics call "earthbound spirits". To the untrained observer they may be hard to tell apart, but you can deal with all manifestations in a similar way.

De-Haunting Exercise

If you believe you have encountered a discarnate human spirit, light a white candle, draw a circle of light around yourself in your mind, and affirm that no spiritual entities may cross the circle. "Speak" to the ghost out loud, or in your mind. Tell the ghost that it is dead, and that its continued presence there may be harmful to living residents.

The most common reaction that you will feel is surprise - most ghosts don't realize that they have died. They linger a long time in a half-suspended state until help comes along. Occasionally you will find that they do realize that they are dead, but that they don't want to leave because they are fearful of leaving physical things (often sex or alcohol) behind, or feel they have not completed some earthly task.

Once you feel that there is understanding, firmly, kindly tell the ghost that it is time to leave. Tell it to look for a spot of light and to focus on it, to move towards it. Encourage it to look for loved ones or angelic helpers. In almost all cases at that point the spirit will leave. If an earthbound spirit ever attempts to attach itself to you, focus your attention on White Light in your heart area and affirm that you do not wish to have that happen. Spirits cannot enter your aura without your permission.

Antiques and Spirits

If you are having persistent problems with hauntings no matter how many times you move, there could be a karmic connection, but it is far more likely you have inadvertently brought a psychic imprint home with you while you were out antiquing.

Imprints are far more common than actual ghosts. They are like an emotional recording imprinted on an object or location. If there is a short impression that repeats itself, if you are not able to achieve a sense of communicating, chances are you are dealing with an imprint.

If you are sensitive, make sure you know the history of any used jewelry or furniture you buy, or avoid the antique stores altogether. If you buy used items, clear them with sage and salt, and affirm that any connection to their past owners is now broken, uncord the item. This does not always work, but it will in most cases. If not, you may have to consider disposing of the item.

For some, it may be best that you stick to all new jewelry, clothing and furniture, at least until you feel comfortable with your experiences, but even new items may carry psychic residue. It is an unfortunate reality that many of the items we purchased are created in sweat-shop conditions, and it is not always possible to avoid buying an item manufactured in this manner (though it is definitely ideal, and not just because you don't want that kind of energy around you). Do a mental cleansing and uncording from any new or used items you buy. Affirm that any past connections are released.

Chapter Twelve
The Circle Meditation

We all have to define our purpose for ourselves, and I find that psychics and creative people often have trouble with this process. Too often we rush through life without truly examining our own needs. Then we wonder why it is we feel unfulfilled and frustrated. Too often as an astrologer I am approached by clients who ask me "What is my Ultimate Purpose in life?"

I myself went from psychic to psychic and they all said things like: "You are a leader, a student, interested in metaphysics, empathic, and want to help people. You enjoy innovative methods of communication, and like being in the spotlight." No one said "You will move to Ontario and become an Internet writer". With the same energies, I could easily have become a psychologist or radio talk-show host. The choice was mine to make ... and I may still explore the other options. When I was considering moving, one of my guides said the following, still very good advice:

"We don't care where you live, where you go. We did not set out your Divine Purpose when you were born. The reason you go to Earth is to discover your Divine Purpose ... to choose it for yourself. Do what makes you happy."

What you need to do is find the Ultimate Answers for yourself. This exercise can help.

Go to the beach, or imagine yourself there, and draw a circle around yourself in the sand. Now, imagine that you can do anything you want to inside the circle. You are happy, prosperous, productive and fulfilled, though you are totally alone inside the circle. Mom, Dad, brothers, sisters, your best friends, "The Joneses", peers and people you barely know, but care about, all are outside the circle, offering their total, unconditional support. Sit inside that feeling for a little while.

Now, think ... what are you doing inside the circle?

You may find yourself doing a lot of things, perhaps just one, but whatever you find yourself doing in that circle is a clue to your purpose.

After you find that purpose, then "reality" has to come in. If you choose to move to another city, or to study certain topics in school, your parents may be hurt or confused. You may have to deal with loneliness and will probably experience money problems (welcome to reality). At least you will have a goal, and an idea of what you want to achieve in life.

Some people are so confused by the demands of other people and of society that they cannot block out the needs of loved-ones, and may find that nothing comes to them inside the circle. Others may find that something outrageous occurs to them that they cannot accept as a practical alternative.

In one session, a client of mine went into her circle, and told me: "I want to watch TV."

I smiled, thinking she must be joking, and said, "Not for the rest of your life, surely!"

"No," she said seriously. "I want to watch TV. It is my only real pleasure in life."

I advised her to look into a career in television. She looked at me like I'd lost my mind. "Seriously," I told her, "There are careers behind the scenes; editing, production, sound manager, etc... why, you could even volunteer to monitor programs for violent acts for a public citizen group!"

She walked away shaking, because she realized for the first time that she had an option to do something she really loved. So do you.

Living With Your Psychic Gifts

Chapter Thirteen
Personal Growth & Psychic Ability

After 20 years of struggling with my psychic abilities, with depression and self-doubt, my good friend John Nemanic offered to sponsor me to attend a little class called "LifeResults" (www.liferesults.org). Little did either of us know how much it would change my life (I believe it saved my life). I had struggled with depression all my life, and I knew my hypersensitivity had something to do with my being miserable all the time, but I didn't know how to get out of my own way.

LifeResults didn't teach me anything I didn't already know. In fact, their "centering" meditation was virtually identical to the Rainbow Lotus Meditation that I'd been teaching in the initial edition of *Living With Your Psychic Gifts* for almost 20 years at that point in time.

Yet something about the process of this particular class struck a chord with me. A week after the class, one of the volunteer team leaders said "Brandi, you're actually smiling!" I protested that I had smiled before, and he replied, "It never reached your eyes until now."

Living With Your Psychic Gifts

In the weeks that followed, I took additional classes, and noticed that not only had my outlook brightened considerably, but I no longer found my psychic abilities as onerous a burden as I had previously. In fact, my intuition seemed to blossom as my sensitivity dropped.

It has been years since that first class, and I have become good friends with class facilitator James Roswell Quinn. I was honored to help him edit his book called "The Love-Based Leader" (www.lovebasedleader.com). While I've had my challenges since then, I have been able to overcome obstacles that would have destroyed me before I took that class. The more I work with the tools I learned in the class, the stronger and sharper my intuition becomes, and yet there are no psychic exercises taught in the class. It is an entirely secular life skills class.

How can that be? I came to realize that the problem I had, the problems most psychics have, is not with our psychic abilities, but with our psyche itself. As intuitives and sensitives we have been trained or have trained ourselves to be servants and victims. We are "supposed" to care for others at the expense of our own well-being. We don't know how to draw boundaries, and we are often struggling with our own emotional wounds from the past.

Living With Your Psychic Gifts

Whenever psychic ability becomes a problem, the core issue is always part physical, part emotional, part mental and part spiritual. Most psychic protection classes focus on the spiritual. We think if we could only make "it" (all the unwanted phenomena) "go away", or block it from coming in, then we'd be okay and happy, the sun would shine again, and everything would be right with the world.

There is actually a chemical way to do that, which apparently works for some folks. It's called Prozac. In addition to making you less sensitive, it also makes you less psychic. The problem is, the drug only masks the problem. It can't bring you joy, at best it can only bring you to what I call "even". You are no longer miserable ... but in my case I could no longer feel anything at all when I took certain anti-depressants. And they were expensive, and the side effects were awful. For me, the "cure" was worse than the problem!

Don't misunderstand me here. There are some people who need medication for their symptoms. I'd never say don't take medications for stress or depression. But the way you look at life definitely makes a difference.

Living With Your Psychic Gifts

Fear, Psychic Experiences and Personal Growth

I have talked to hundreds of people about their fears. They often approach me full of anxiety and fears, not sure if they are "going crazy", and desperate to make it all "go away".

If that sounds familiar, can I ask you what may sound like an odd question? Why are you so scared about this? Go deeper. Be honest with yourself. Since being afraid can't change a thing, why do we do it? Why do we let ourselves stay scared?

For a moment, take a pen and a piece of paper, and write down all the reasons you are afraid of your psychic abilities. What is the worst case scenario?

It usually comes down to a few different possibilities: (you may be able to come up with more)

• The myth that the unknown is innately scary. If the unknown was all that scary, no child would go exploring. Think about all the times you were afraid about something new, then discovered it was something you really liked!

Living With Your Psychic Gifts

- We are afraid of going "crazy". Since fear is at the heart of insanity does it make any sense whatsoever to pump up our adrenaline with fears about going nuts?
- Being scared gets attention, makes others take our feelings more seriously. Many people don't like to admit this, but we all can point to someone else who we think is a drama queen.
- Fear is a bonding mechanism. A scary story shared between friends can bring you closer together. The problem is, repeating the story over and over in a fearful manner only reinforces the fear.
- We may be afraid of being "different". Human beings are tribal animals, and anything that makes us seem different in our own eyes or the eyes of others, we come to fear. But life would be pretty boring if no one had the courage to be unique, or to share their gifts.
- Movies are powerful things, they are designed to be dramatic and scary, and when the only experience people have of the spirit world is movies, it's no wonder so many of us are scared sick when these things happen.

I can understand why psychic experiences may be frightening in the moment. The question I have is why do you continue to fear it? Why do you bring that fear into the rest of your day, and out into your life? Go deeper on this one, it could be valuable. If you face something fearful, there are only two options: either you can do something about it or you cannot. If you can do something about it, do that thing. If you cannot, then accept it is happening. There is no point to fear in this situation. It's just a voice. It cannot actually harm you ... unless you permit yourself to be so frightened that you endanger yourself with your own fears! When you think about it like that, it takes some of the sting out of it.

It may take a while before you may be able to have one of these experiences without reacting with fear. Maybe there will always be some fear. My "sleep paralysis" experiences come rarely now, but they are occasionally ugly, and sometimes I still react with fear. Once I am fully awake, I put my feet and hands in cold water, I cuddle my cat, I listen to some music until I feel better (if you are religious, maybe read some religious literature or the Bible for a while). The more I have done this, the easier and more quickly I get past my fear. It's like a muscle, I have to keep exercising it to keep strong.

If you are truly fearful for your sanity, then you need to seek medical advice. If you have a good relationship with your doctor and feel you have trust there, then maybe you would get some comfort from talking about this experience. If that's what you fear most, and ruling that out could be a huge relief.

Chapter Fourteen
Doing Readings, Going Professional

Now that you are comfortable with your psychic gifts, you feel in control, you probably want to share them with others. Some of you may decide to enter the world of "professional psychics", and some may be horrified by the idea. But many of you are going to want to share your insights or do "readings" for your family and friends, and whether you do so for money or out of love, there are some pitfalls and roadblocks you have to consider.

I could write a whole new book about marketing and self-promotion for psychics, and maybe someday I will. But for now let's just cover the basics you need to consider before you get into the business of reading for others, whether for fun or profit.

Seek permission, wait to be asked

For professionals and non-professionals alike it is important to remember not to offer advice, feedback, insights or share visions with others if you haven't been asked, and to never do "healing" work on others without their permission. I don't even pray for specific outcomes for others without getting their express permission.

There are many reasons for this. You could be wrong about what you see, especially when you first start out. And whether or not you are right, some people often give unsolicited advice considerably less value than opinions they have sought out. Others will give your advice too much credence because of the psychic source. With prayer and healing, we often put our own desires into our intentions, and this can have unintended and negative side effects.

One time I was suffering headaches and having awful nightmares about my family being attacked by demons. I spoke to a loved one and discovered she'd been praying for me to return to the faith. She was terrified that I had demons around me. So I asked her to instead pray that "God's will be done", a compromise we could both live with. The headaches and nightmares ended. Her intentions were honorable, but the outcome was harmful. If you are asked to pray for or send energy to someone you don't know, or wish to help an ailing loved one whose permission you cannot obtain, affirm that whatever is best for them, in their highest good, and in accordance with their will and desires will be the thing that comes to pass. Don't specify an outcome. Let that be their choice.

Study, Study, Study

Whatever tool, technique or oracle you use, study it for a period of time, and do a lot of journal writing before you offer "readings" to others, whether you are "going pro" or are simply reading across the supper table. People will tend to give your psychic pronouncements greater weight than they will ordinary advice. You have a responsibility to know what you are talking about.

Study yourself. Your reactions, fears, biases and beliefs will affect your accuracy. Are you really sharing the energy of a psychic insight with a loved one, or are you hiding your desires behind a mystic cloak? Is your sister's new boyfriend really giving you the psychic creeps or do you simply not like him? Make sure you don't abuse the authority that this gift can bring you.

Study other psychics, like James Van Praagh. Notice how they come across. You'll notice that the more respected psychics insist that the client tell them as little as possible before a reading, that they educate clients as to the limits of what they can sense, and that they are always gentle when breaking bad news to a client.

Volunteer at a crisis clinic, study psychology, philosophy, religions, and study the basics of crisis intervention. If you do readings professionally you'll occasionally encounter people who are unstable, mentally ill, even suicidal. If you don't know how to handle this you can do more harm than good.

Dealing With Bad News

When I first started reading, I had the good fortune to start off with practical advice, a strong dose of common sense and guidance from some highly professional psychics. I had a background that well prepared me for dealing with challenging situations. But I quickly realized others were not so fortunate. To this day, I regularly meet people who have had the misfortune to come across an unprofessional psychic who scared the daylights out of them.

"She stopped the reading cold when the Death card came up, and wouldn't tell me anything!" the clients ask me, eyes bright with terror and unshed tears. "Then she took all the cards off the table and left me just sitting there! Am I evil or something? Does the Death Card really mean someone is going to die?"

This is almost never the case. Whether it is the Death Card, or the Ace of Spades, or an unfortunate astrological aspect, the darkest of omens usually indicate that a significant change is coming – but accidental or unanticipated death is notoriously hard to predict. The only time it legitimately comes up in a reading is when it is expected.

Say you have a client whose mother who is ill and getting ready to cross. That's something legitimate to mention, with some tact and consideration. You can say, "I think you have an elder female relative who is suffering from a health problem (specify if you can what that health problem feels like). Is that correct?" If so, it may be legitimate to gently suggest that she getting ready to cross over.

You never just bluntly say, "I think the old bird's time is up." And you never close up the reading shivering with fear, afraid to tell your client the bad news – because whatever it is, it's guaranteed to be not nearly so bad as it will become in their imaginations if you leave them hanging. If you don't know how to tactfully handle such a revelation, either ignore it, or move to other topics, or reconsider whether or not you are fit to advise others at all.

I have had clients ask me if they are evil, if they are demon possessed, and if they or their loved ones are doomed to some horrible fate. All because an unprofessional psychic made a huge deal out of the Death Card. They have suffered in quiet terror for years in some cases. This sort of behavior is unprofessional, abusive, wrong and cowardly. If you don't know the cards, or fear a particular card this much, then don't read for others. Not even for your friends.

There are going to be times when you come across truly negative people that you can't read. It is your responsibility to be as honest as you can, without blaming or being judgmental. Tell them you can't read for them right now, that your vibrations are not harmonious, that you think they might have better luck with someone else. Ninety-nine times out of a hundred this will be true. I recall one fellow I worked with often had this problem. He was forever bringing women to me that he could not read. Invariably they would turn out to come from horribly abusive backgrounds, often suffering in present-day abusive partnerships. I had no problem reading them, they were not "evil" people. They just had an experience he could not cope with or relate to, and that was fine. Energies that seem harsh or negative to one psychic might be more understandable to another.

Living With Your Psychic Gifts

Responsibility

Make sure you understand what your responsibility is and what lays with the person you are reading for. Don't let yourself be turned into anyone's "coin toss". Often, when choices are hard, people will turn over their power to a psychic with the question "What should I do?" Ultimately, they have to be the ones to make that decision. It can be flattering when someone so values your advice that they follow it without question, but that's a trap for both of you. You don't want to be anyone's guru. You are as human as they are, as prone to make mistakes. Outline the energy, how you think it will manifest, depending on their choices, then insist that they be the ones to make the final choice.

To charge or not to charge

It's unbelievable that we're still arguing this point, but there are some folks who think it is "unspiritual" or "negative" to charge money for psychic advice. I've usually found this sort of silly nonsense coming from folks who can more than afford the cost of a basic reading, people who don't have to struggle themselves to make ends meet.

If I bother to argue the point, I will ask them what they do, and if they get paid for their "gifts". Then I may ask if they are paying their local pastor for his services (some are shocked to find out that's where part of the collection plate money is going). I also ask whether or not they think their doctor's healing gift is "too spiritual" to be valued in monetary terms.

If you do choose to go into this professionally, if you feel your gift is calling out for this expression, you act in a professional manner, keep your knowledge up to date, and charge a fair market value, you don't have to apologize to anyone for asking a fee. No one ever died for lack of psychic advice. If anyone is "sinning" on this score it is more than certainly the doctors, pharmacists and psychiatrists, whose fees are often outrageous and whose skills, gifts, talents and services are unarguably "life or death". And if you feel this is a spiritual gift you are called to share freely ... bless you. That is your choice.

Things you can't charge for

Be aware of the laws in your country, province or state. There may be services you cannot charge for. In parts of the USA, believe it or not, charging for astrological readings is illegal. In Canada it is prudent to have a sign or disclaimer in your advertising that says, "Readings are for fun and entertainment purposes only", because there is a small subsection in the Canadian Criminal Code that says, "You may not pretend to tell the future".

I do not charge for "blessings", "house clearings" or any form of "ritual-based" service. I ask only that travel expenses be covered, and will accept a donation to cover my time. I suggest that the client pay whatever they are paid for the same time period, in order to be fair. I'll take more, if they want to express gratitude this way, but it's not suggested or asked for. Usually, I will suggest to clients that they can do these things themselves, I'll offer to show them how, but sometimes there is a persistent energy, and they want a pro to tackle it.

The reason I don't charge a set fee for such a process is that I cannot guarantee an outcome. I also don't want to get mixed up with or lumped into that group of evil-doers who charge money for lifting curses and other bogus scams. These people give us all a bad name. I do charge for my time and expenses, otherwise I could not afford to do this kind of work at all. I feel it's a fair trade, and clients are always notified in advance that I will do my best. But when you are dealing with spirits especially, it is hard to know in advance whose willpower will turn out to be strongest, and there is no objective way to test my efficacy.

Remember to Ground and Protect

Before and after every reading ground yourself, and re-affirm your circle of protection. Make sure there is a firm "start" and "finish" to the process. This will help keep your "psychic" life separate from the "mundane", and ensures you are not walking around with your aura wide open, inviting unknown energies to fly in all the time.

Doing readings at home

I don't recommend this, unless you have a dedicated space, ideally with its own entrance. Because you will be dragging energy into your living quarters from the business, and some of that energy will be less than pleasant. If you must do so, make sure to clear your home after every reading.

Record your readings

Whether you read at home or at an expo, you will need to have a recorder and a method to deliver your recordings to your clients. You may choose to allow clients to record readings on their mobile phones, or offer to send digital recordings to them later via email. But you should always offer to record your sessions.

Psychic Fairs, Expos

If you decide to "go pro", you may decide to try out the local "Psychic Expo". There are some pros and cons. You'll definitely meet people you could not have met otherwise, and if things are slow enough, chat with them and learn from them about their own psychic experiences.

Don't expect to make a lot of money at these shows. The going rate is between $30-$100 per reading, but your overhead is going to be terrific. It's between $250-$800 per booth for 3 days on average, and that's not counting the food (bring your own, show food is universally awful), lodging and travel expenses. Most psychics only do shows in their home towns, but there are a few "roadies" who sleep in camper-vans and travel cross-country. Often they are retirees who do it more for love than money.

I recommend that you do the local shows, or shows within driving distance, but that you focus your promotional efforts on getting into the press, setting up an office, establishing a social media presence and creating a web site (see www.bizangel.ca if you need help getting set up). The shows will bring you greater success if you think of them as promotional rather than sales events. You want to make money if you can, but their greatest power is to bring people into your office after the show.

Be Professional

My primary gripe with many psychics at expos and fairs is that they don't present a minimally polished, professional image. These days, computers are common, and there is no excuse with having sloppy literature or signage. Not to mention this will adversely affect your business. Have business cards. Put together a flyer. And for goodness sakes, at least have a Facebook page if not a web site of your own. Nothing screams "unprofessional" like sloppy materials.

It is not only in dress, signage and advertising that you must remember to be professional. The biggest gripe of show promoters is the unprofessional behavior they have to tolerate amongst their exhibitors. Yes, we do tend to be creative and spontaneous, but that is no excuse for violating contracts, showing up late, leaving early, failure to pay on time, demands for special treatment or verbal abuse of staff for situations they cannot control (like electricity or signage which are usually handled by contractors).

On Being Wrong – Predictions versus Forecasting

I have been known to say that in some of my best readings, my predictions were dead wrong.

The true value of the readings were not in the predictions I made for the future. Rather, the value lay in the clear reflection to the client of her life now, and what she needed to change, in order to make it better. I might predict disaster in a relationship, but if certain attitudes, ideas or habits are changed, then the outcome may be quite different. The whole point to developing your gift is to become more self aware, and to assist other people along that path.

Some developing psychics treat being "wrong" in their predictions as the end of the world. If their insights aren't right 100% of the time, they start the second-guessing all over again, falling back into fearful patterns and anxiety.

A little skepticism is a good thing. It keeps us on our toes. Journaling is in part designed to catch our mistakes and guide us to a more accurate and controlled use of our abilities.

Remember that having a psychic gift does not make you omniscient. You'll be stunningly wrong from time to time. That does not mean that you are "crazy", "imagining things" or that you are kidding yourself. It may be so – and it is good you keep that possibility in mind as a reality check, but in many cases it is not the psychic energy that is to blame when you are "wrong", it is your own interpretation that is off.

I remember one time when I was working in a psychic fair, and was approached by the local media, asked to "predict" the outcome of a local election. What I sensed on the energy level was a massive upset – a stunning outcome that would have all the pundits reeling. The only outcome that would surprise me would be the incumbents pulling of a victory, so certain seemed their defeat. So I predicted that they would win. Another psychic, asked "Who will win, Party A or Party B" cryptically responded "Neither." Yet this seemed impossible, and she indicated she was confused about the outcome.

What actually happened was that the third party pulled off an amazing and totally unexpected "come from behind" advance that nearly upset the favored candidates, and knocking the incumbents almost completely off the map. The favored party did win – but only just barely, with a few seats to spare.

If I had stuck to the "energy" I sensed, instead of trying to interpret it, I would have been right. But because I tried to interpret how that energy would manifest, my own preconceptions got in the way, and the actual prediction came out totally wrong. This is the most common way that psychic predictions fail. If you journal regularly it is one of the patterns you'll begin to see in your own thought processes. You'll learn the difference between the "forecast", the "psychic energy" and the "prediction", the "manifestation" or "outcome". As a responsible psychic, professional or not, it is important that you understand the difference, and explain this to people you encounter as a psychic.

One of the reasons there is so much derision of psychics these days is that too many of us, both professional and "amateur", is that we tend to make "predictions" not forecasts.

Here is an example of the difference between a "forecast" and a "prediction".

Forecast: "I sense a strong energy involving children around you, and feel that at this specific time that you are going to be more involved with children, or there will be changes involving children in your life."

Prediction: "You are going to have a baby next year."

The prediction seems a little more precise than the forecast, but it may be totally wrong. The energy could also manifest as the other person taking up a teaching job, or having a new cousin, niece or nephew. Unless the energy comes to you in a very specific form, don't try to second-guess it.

Some skeptics say this is a dodge, allowing for other ways to account for mistakes, but that's not the case. I am not suggesting you be more vague. In fact I am suggesting you be more precise about exactly what it is you are seeing and sensing, and that includes acknowledging its limits.

The fact is that certain outcomes cannot reliably be predicted.

On that point the skeptics and I are in perfect agreement. When you see a psychic who is claiming to be able to predict your future with absolutely certainty, or meet someone who makes exaggerated claims about being able to predict events, you almost always find someone who is on the fringes mentally and professionally.

Psychic ability can be used to enhance your life. You'll tune into things at times, and feel that there is no way you could have known them. But for the most part what you will experience is an extension of, an enhancement of your intuitive ability, not a clear and open window to the minds of others, or a cosmic TV screen that tells you in perfect clarity the whims of fate.

Living With Your Psychic Gifts

Glossary

Akashic Records or Akasha - the underlying vibration of physical reality, or collective human consciousness, which holds within it a holographic record of the past, present, and (perhaps) the future. Some psychics claim to tap this source directly, and to "read" it as if it were some sort of book or holographic recording.

Astral Plane or Level - A level of existence that many psychics believe is closely related to the dream plane of consciousness. Whether this is a physical dimension close to our own or a dimension of human consciousness is in dispute.

Astral Travel - The ability to consciously travel out of the body for periods of time. Most of these experiences take place on the astral plane.

Astrology - The study of the positions of the stars, planets, asteroids, and other extra-terrestrial bodies and their relationship to events and people on Earth.

Aura - The field of energy that envelops and may direct the health and shape of the human body.

Living With Your Psychic Gifts

Chakras - "Wheels" of energy that align the subtle bodies. There are said to be 7 chakras in most belief systems.

Channel - Similar to a medium, channelers may contact and speak for the spirits of the dead, nature spirits, and entities that have claimed to be extra-terrestrial in origin.

Divination - The use of an oracle or device to foretell the future, and in modern times often used as a tool of self-discovery.

Earth-Bound Spirit - A spirit of a human (sometimes an animal) that is "stuck" in the physical plane. For assistance, please refer to The Unquiet Dead by Edith Fiore (see psychicprotection.net/recommended-reading).

Elements - Fire, Air, Water and Earth - The four cornerstones of most metaphysical systems.

Empath - A person with the ability to sense other people's emotions. Most "sensitives" are not just psychic but empathic as well.

Karma - The belief that one's actions in this lifetime will be balanced out by reward or punishment in future lives. Personally I don't believe that is how it works, I believe what we see as karmic is more a reflection of more basic cause and effect due to habitual reaction cycles.

Kundalini - The energy at the base of the spine which can be aroused during intense meditation, but which may also be aroused in some individuals seemingly by accident.

Medium - A person with the ability to contact the spirits of the dead.

NDE – "Near Death Experience".

Numerology - The study of the esoteric meaning of numbers.

Occult - "Hidden" knowledge, information that is available only to a select few initiates. Every religion, including Christianity, has an "occult" branch.

OOBE - "Out of Body Experience".

Oracle - A person or a tool that is used to gain wisdom or to foretell the future. Tarot cards for example are often referred to as an oracle.

Ouija - A board game, consisting of a printed board with the letters of the alphabet and a pointer or planchet. Two or more players place their hands on the pointer and invite spirits to "speak" through the board. It is highly recommended that beginners do **NOT** play with the Ouija board.

Pagan - Literally "non-Christian" - Pagan beliefs can be anything that is not mainstream Christian belief at any point in history. Modern pagans tend to be nature and goddess worshippers. "Pagan" in ancient times generally referred to the beliefs of the Romans, Egyptians and Greeks, then later to the indigenous beliefs of the Celts, Europeans and Norse.

Palmistry - The study of the lines and features of the human hand, and their relation to human personality, health and behavior.

Precognition - The ability to foretell the future via any number of psychic skills.

Psychometry - The ability to sense thoughts, feelings and to relive events by handling personal items (usually jewelry) or by touching other people.

Satanism - An inversion of Christian beliefs, largely reinvented in the 20th century as a polemical rebellion.

Living With Your Psychic Gifts

Sensitives - People with the ability to sense other people's emotions or thoughts to a frequently uncomfortable degree.

Silver Cord - A cord of energy that ties the astral body to the physical body. It is seen often during astral travel and it is believed that it is broken at death.

Tarot Cards - A group of 78 cards, split into 22 Major Arcana, and 56 Numbered cards, the precursor to modern playing cards, which date back to the 1600's and are used in divination.

Telepathy - The ability to read the thoughts of other people.

Wicca - A religion of nature and goddess worship, often referred to as "witchcraft". Those calling themselves "witches" are not always involved in Wicca, but most Wiccans call themselves witches.

Recommended Reading

As the bibliography is constantly being updated and changed, it is kept online. To order recommended books, or to view the most up to date list, please click on "Recommended Reading" at www.psychicprotection.net.

Selected Links:

www.psychicprotection.net
www.facebook.com/psychicprotection
twitter.com/bjasmine
www.linkedin.com/in/bjasmine
www.youtube.com/user/bjasmine

Astrology.ca

Biz Angel: www.bizangel.ca

LifeResults: www.lifesresults.org

John Nemanic: www.johnnemanic.com

James Roswell Quinn: www.lovebasedleader.com

Jasmine's Gallery: www.bjasmine.com

Living With Your Psychic Gifts

Living With Your Psychic Gifts

www.ingramcontent.com/pod-product-compliance
Lightning Source LLC
Chambersburg PA
CBHW060513090426
42735CB00011B/2207